THE OUTSTANDING FACTOR

Concepts in Quality Investing

Victori Capital

Victori Capital

.

ISBN-10: 1727450884
ISBN-13: 978-1727450880

CONTENTS

PART III: COGNITIVE BIASES

FOREWORD

The Outstanding Factor was originally published as a collection of monthly letters written by Victori Capital from August 2014 through April 2017. The letters covered a broad range of topics that we consider relevant to understanding the way we invest. Our quest for the outstanding relates mostly to management, businesses, and industries, but the concepts that we study and apply come from a wide array of fields and disciplines.

In this second edition of our book, we reorganized the chapters based on their topics, instead of by the chronological order of the letters. We believe this format better conveys the timelessness of the concepts discussed, while also enabling us to improve the flow of ideas and enhance the reader's understanding of the topics and how they relate to our philosophy of investing.

Victori Capital

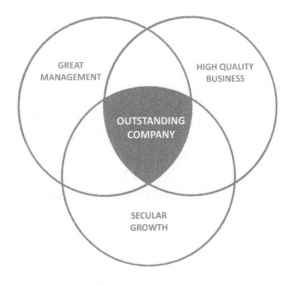

Victori Capital is an asset manager that invests in companies that are selected to meet high standards with respect to quality of management, financial performance, and durability of growth. By focusing on Outstanding Companies, we aim to capture the long-term wealth creation that occurs when great managements of high-quality businesses seize attractive secular growth opportunities. For more information visit www.victoricapital.com.

PART I

INVESTING

THE OUTSTANDING FACTOR

1   PREDICTION

"Prediction is very difficult, especially if it's about the future."

Niels Bohr

We could not think of a better topic with which to begin this book than our philosophy of focusing on what is knowable. While we realize it is relevant to follow current events and track macro developments, we do not believe it is knowable how interest rates will fluctuate, when the Fed will act, or when buyers will out-weigh sellers in the short term. We do believe, however, that we can know with a good dose of confidence that a reputable CEO with a stellar track record, or an outstanding company with a culture of innovation and repeatable processes, will create outsized value over time. Finding these attributes and establishing their staying power is what drives us to invest.

One of the best books on investing that we ever read isn't an investment book at all. It is called *The Signal and the Noise* and was written by Nate Silver, the famous American statistician who is known for accurately predicting the outcome of elections and sports tournaments.[1] While Nate is guilty of predicting that Brazil would win the 2014 World Cup, his insights on how to use information are invaluable nonetheless. Through historical examples dating back to the invention of the printing press in 1440 to that of the World Wide Web in 1990, he makes the case that we face great danger whenever information growth outpaces our understanding of how to process it. As he concludes, "We have a prediction problem. We love to predict things – and we aren't very good at it."

The notion of predicting, or forecasting, is of critical importance to investing, so we are not suggesting that we ignore it. We certainly have our views on where the economy may be headed, or how an industry cycle will play out, and we incorporate these views into the financial models that we build for our companies. In that sense, we are no different from the next guy who's trying to guess the future. The problem is not in the attempt at forecasting by itself, but in the misapplication of those forecasts, or better yet, the false sense of confidence that the numbers produce. This effect on investors is so prevalent that the behavioral finance academics have come up with a scientific term for it: the "illusion of knowledge" bias.

Howard Marks, the founder of Oaktree Capital, dedicated an entire chapter to this topic in his book, *The Most Important Thing*, which he titled *Knowing What You Don't Know*.[2] He classifies investors into two groups: the "I Know" school, and the "I Don't Know" school – and he contends that most investors he has met over the years belong to the "I know" school. These are people who think that knowledge of the future direction of economies, interest rates, and markets is essential for investment success, and they are confident this can be achieved. While they don't often get their picture in the papers, those who belong to the "I Don't Know" school tend to make better investments over time, since they recognize that you can't know the future, and that the proper goal is to do the best job in the absence of that knowledge.

To quote Marks, "whatever limitations are imposed on us in the investment world, it's a heck of a lot better to acknowledge them and accommodate than to deny them and forge ahead". While the ranks of market strategists, economists, and so-called "experts" keeps multiplying, they do not offer solutions. The study we have seen most quoted on this very question is that by Philip Tetlock, who tracked 284 experts that made 82,361 forecasts on politics and economics over a period of years.[3] The study concludes that the alleged experts are even less accurate than non-experts in guessing what will happen, as they were wrong more than half the time. Although one needs to be reasonably informed on a subject to make credible predictions, the study found that being a true "expert" or a "guru" actually makes someone a less reliable forecaster. The more facts, information, and history an expert knows, the more likely he is to develop pet theories or biases that will taint his forecasting judgment.

So, if relying on expert forecasts and market predictions is not the answer, then what is? In our view, the answer rests on a concentration and focus on smaller picture, repeatable factors. This view is what compels us to devote the majority of our effort towards identifying strong managements, solid companies, and secular growth themes. It is not to say that we invest oblivious to the macro picture, as that would be foolish. However, we follow a disciplined process that identifies investments based on these more knowable attributes, instead of where the overall market is headed.

In subsequent chapters we will address in more detail how we approach the subject of price, but it would be disingenuous to end this discussion without a single mention of it. We consider ourselves value investors, so we do not merely look for outstanding companies and great managements regardless of price. What sets us apart from most value investors is that we don't lead with price. Instead of looking to buy on the cheap, we view price more as a part of the risk analysis than anything else. Our definition of bargain is the company that can produce solid returns repeatedly, to an extent that is under-appreciated by the market. The value we seek to add as investors comes from identifying and owning such outstanding companies while they compound at above-market rates. We tend to be more interested in the value that is created outside of the market, at the individual company level, where the importance of predictions is less relevant, and the forecasts themselves are easier to make.

2   VALUE CREATION

"Shareholder value is a result, not a strategy."

Jack Welch

As the quote above implies, *value* and *value creation strategies* are distinct concepts that are often in conflict. Many of the actions undertaken for the sake of unlocking value to reward current shareholders end up compromising future value, while less popular decisions that do not reward today's shareholders can turn out to be the ones that add the most value in the outer years. This tradeoff between short-term pain and long-term gain is the essence of investing.

In his 2016 book titled *Investment: A History*, Norton Reamer, the former CEO of Putnam, writes:

"Investment management is all about asset pricing, and each manager brings to the task his or her own theories of value. So, while there is more to do in the academic arena, we will never resolve a theory of value that is universal and perfect – that, after all, is the very art of investing."[4] Indeed, investors come in many forms. Some find value in turnarounds and distressed situations while others focus on outsized growth. While the mandates and timeframes of these different types of investors can vary widely, those of company managements tend to be more constant. As stewards of shareholder capital and guardians of the franchises that they lead, company managements must look after the well-being of all constituents, including employees and customers, over a much longer timeframe (i.e. perpetuity) than most modern investors are willing to commit. This divergence of purpose explains many of the battles between otherwise strong managements and their more demanding shareholders.

Another argument against shareholder-value-creation mandates was proposed by John Kay. In his 2010 book titled *Obliquity: How Our Goals are Best Achieved Indirectly*, he observes: "The wealthiest people are not those most assertive in the pursuit of wealth. The greatest paintings are not the most accurate representations of their subjects; the forests most resistant to fires are not the ones whose foresters are best at putting out fires."[5] One of the key themes in his book is that, in complex social systems like markets, families, and corporations, there is no predictable connection between intentions and outcomes. Shareholder value is not necessarily the result of shareholder-friendly actions, just as happiness is not the aggregation of happy moments. He claims that some of the most successful companies in history, such as Boeing, Microsoft, Walmart, Google, and Amazon, did not achieve their greatness by focusing directly on profits, and certainly not short-term accounting profits. They all had a bigger purpose that guided their actions. To paraphrase Jack Welch, outsized shareholder value creation was the result, not the strategy.

In his criticism of companies that focus on creating shareholder value as their main purpose, Kay goes on to question the existence of a true measure of profit. "Anyone who has thought hard about the matter," he claims, "knows that the quest for the true measure of profit is as illusory as the search for a measure of poetic perfection." Indeed, after teaching economics for decades and authoring several notable books on the topic, Professor Kay admits that he has never resolved the question of what constitutes a true profit. The sustained dispersion of earnings multiples across markets is proof that equal profit streams can have vastly different values. The implication is that financial models and accounting metrics alone cannot by themselves determine value. Management quality, culture, repeatability, and the overall attractiveness of the business are also critical determinants of worth.

Not everyone agrees with John Kay's oblique approach to value creation. In 2013, Professor Kevin Kaiser, of INSEAD, authored a book titled *The Blue Line Imperative*, where he asserts that: "Value creation, when properly understood, is not simply someone's ethical perspective on how to manage a company. Value creation is a self-generating, self-governing, basic planetary imperative based on nature itself, and if you don't uphold it, the planet shuts you down every time."[6] While his observation might hold true with the benefit of hindsight, it is not very helpful to the investor who seeks to pick the few companies that will create outsized shareholder value in the future. Not every company knows what to do to drive long-term value, and many are in fact motivated by short-term incentives. A focused pursuit of value, or happiness, is a great motivator, but it is rarely the core driver of greatness. From Walt Disney to Steve Jobs, the day-to-day lives of the greatest achievers are rarely about happiness and reward. The reality seems to be that value often accrues to those who are willing to endure long periods of outsized suffering in exchange for an unknown future gain.

In summary, actions that reward current holders often make little economic sense to long-term investors. While a keen sense and appreciation for value creation is an important attribute of outstanding companies, it is rarely a catalyst. At Victori Capital, the opportunity that we seek to capture is less about the maximization of short-term gain and more about the underappreciation of future value creation.

3 SWARM INTELLIGENCE

*"Talent wins games, but teamwork and intelligence
win championships."*

Michael Jordan

The core of our investment strategy is an unwavering focus on not just companies, but on *outstanding* companies run by *outstanding* people. We pay close attention to strong leadership because, without it, we believe it is impossible for companies to harness the power of intelligent organization. This collective intelligence that great companies possess is as hard to detect as it is to measure, but we believe it is behind some of the best investment opportunities in the market.

The book *Repeatability,* published in March 2012 by Bain & Company, claims that while external forces such as industry dynamics and business cycles play a role in the success of organizations, a company's fate is most influenced by its own actions.[7] In their study of what they call "great repeatable models", the authors describe not only companies that are still known to be great, but also those that were once great and failed because of their inability to adapt to a changing environment. This book has shaped our thinking of what really matters to investors, and it has also helped sharpen our focus on sustainable compounding.

The challenge faced by investors, but not necessarily by management consultants, is that stocks will often reflect a perception of greatness that most companies simply do not possess (i.e. the *halo effect*). In other words, simply buying stocks of companies that have done well, without regard to sustainability and continuous improvement, can lead to disappointing results when conditions change. On the flip side, there are companies that prove to be considerably more formidable than the market ever appreciates – and those are the ones we really like. Such companies do not seem as spectacular on the surface, but like ant colonies, they are adaptive and practically unstoppable in their pursuits. They tend to possess a high degree of *swarm intelligence*.

The expression *swarm intelligence* was first used in a 1988 scientific paper by researchers of cellular robotics who were interested in modeling the sophisticated "self-organizing" behavior of ant colonies. While ants are not that clever individually, ant colonies are highly adaptive and very efficient. "If you watch an ant try to accomplish something, you'll be impressed by how inept it is," says Deborah M. Gordon, a biologist at Stanford University, in an interview with *National Geographic* on swarm theory.[8] She continues: "Ants aren't smart, ant colonies are. A colony can solve problems unthinkable for individual ants, such as finding the shortest path to the best food source, allocating workers to different tasks, or defending a territory from neighbors. As individuals, ants might be tiny dummies, but as colonies, they respond quickly and effectively to their environment."

Certainly, the individuality and talents of employees matter more than that of ants, but great companies tend to have a lot more in common with ant colonies than meets the eye. When individuals share a common vision, and when they behave within a set of simple rules, they are essentially borrowing from swarm theory. A leader who forms a simple vision that is disseminated consistently to all levels of the organization is perhaps the most important driver of not only corporate success, but of military and athletic endeavors as well. As we have seen time and again in sports, when a coach's strategy is unclear, even a team of world-class players can fail miserably.

Real-life examples of the power of swarm intelligence in human experience are perhaps most prominent in military history, where the successful commanders were those who knew how to shorten the distance between themselves and the front line. Horatio Nelson, for instance, who was a British flag officer in the Royal Navy during the late 1700s, was noted for his inspirational leadership and grasp of strategy. Long before the term *swarm intelligence* was coined, Nelson employed the theory to achieve decisive naval victories that changed the course of history. He organized his men into independent colonies of warriors by training them on what he called simple truths. His strategy produced task forces capable of executing complex missions independently, making them consistently nimbler and more effective than their enemies.

The authors of *Repeatability* demonstrate through numerous examples, and a vast body of research, that most companies are ill-equipped to benefit from swarm intelligence, due to lack of awareness. They cite surveys of multiple levels of employees across thousands of organizations to support their claim that companies in general lack self-awareness, even at the executive level. This is where the parallel between corporations and ant colonies breaks down.

When we study a company and its leaders, we look for signs of swarm intelligence. We ask ourselves if the CEO has a convincing and simple message that the entire organization can understand. Is the organization self-aware? A company with high swarm intelligence can often change CEOs without skipping a beat, since everyone already knows the direction. They are also capable of reacting to competitive and economic threats with unimaginable speed and effectiveness. These are the sort of traits that make companies *outstanding*.

Swarm intelligence is not the only quality attribute we focus on, but it is one that we consider very important, especially since it is often underestimated by investors. We pay attention to industries as well, particularly the ones that benefit from secular trends, and we look forward to discussing those in subsequent chapters.

4   GROUP DYNAMICS

"Attitude is a little thing that makes a big difference."

Winston Churchill

Group dynamics is of paramount importance in investing as well as in the general pursuit of excellence. Like markets, the behavior of groups is complex, heavily biased, and difficult to predict. As is the case with most complex systems, the performance of groups follows a power law, with a few achieving extraordinary results while most others struggle to make a difference. We believe that there are common attributes among the elite groups of exceptional performers. Whether in sports, business, or investing, group dynamics is often the main driver of some of the most extraordinary outcomes in history, as well as some of the most outstanding companies.

In *Leading at the Edge*, Dennis Perkins, a Vietnam War veteran and professor at the Yale School of Management, profiles the dramatic account of Ernest Shackleton's Antarctica expedition from the viewpoint of a management consultant.[9]   One of the several prescriptions that he offers leaders for maximizing the performance of their teams is to establish an egalitarian spirit that fosters a feeling of inclusion regardless of rank.   When all team members feel a sense of involvement, positive outcomes are more likely to come about.

To reinforce this norm of equal treatment, Shackleton made sure that he, as the leader of the expedition, got no special privileges.   He wore the same clothing, ate the same food, and took his turn in the rotation of daily chores.   Perkins recounts the story of when their ship, the Endurance, broke up and the men found themselves with fewer reindeer-skin sleeping bags than they needed.   To ensure equal treatment, the desirable bags were distributed using a lottery in which Shackleton did not participate.   Unlike the famous explorer Robert Falcon Scott, who gave orders and observed while his men labored, Shackleton was an integral part of the team, and he reinforced this culture by example.   While chance may have played a role, Perkins speculates that the outcome of Scott's disastrous journey to the South Pole, where he and his entire crew died, could be attributed to his inferior, command-and-control management style, borrowed from the Royal British Navy. In times of crisis, when teamwork becomes most critical, a team whose members feel excluded and unfairly treated falls apart.

Dr. Christopher Ahmad, an accomplished orthopedic surgeon who is the head physician of the New York Yankees, recently published a book titled *Skill*, in which he discusses the key principles that surgeons, athletes and other elite performers use to achieve mastery.[10] He claims that the ability to keep reaching for improvement is central to the mastery of a skill, and one of the principles he proposes, which relates to group dynamics, is to praise effortful practice, not good results. "Early praise," writes Dr. Ahmad, "can create complacency or even fear of underachievement or failing to meet expectations, which thereby undermines the process of reaching." Dr. Ahmad's thesis regarding early praise was confirmed in an experiment performed by Carol Dweck of Harvard University. A group of fifth graders were given a series of puzzles to work on. Then they were given their scores and six words of praise, either "You must be smart at this!" or "You must have worked really hard." All students were given a second test and given a choice of whether they wanted to take a hard test or an easy test. Remarkably, a full two-thirds of students praised for being smart took the easy test, while ninety percent of the effort-praised kids took the hard test. When good results occur, outstanding coaches and business leaders alike tend to praise in such ways that the team members are inspired to keep reaching instead of relaxing.

Another important attribute of extraordinary teams is that they can operate in a state of *flow*. Wikipedia defines flow as "the mental state of operation in which a person performing an activity is fully immersed in a feeling of energized focus, full involvement, and enjoyment in the process of the activity." Named by psychology professor Mihály Csíkszentmihályi, the concept has been widely referenced across a variety of fields, but has existed for thousands of years under other guises.[11]

A 1989 paper by Hamilton College sociology professor Daniel Chambliss offers a good example of the role that flow plays in achieving outstanding results.[12] From January 1983 to August 1984, Professor Chambliss attended a series of national and international class swimming events conducted by United States Swimming Inc., the national governing body for the sport. He studied the prevalence and development of excellence in the sport cross-sectionally (looking at all levels of the sport) and longitudinally (over a span of careers). He found that true excellence had less to do with actual skill than with attitude. "At the higher levels of competitive swimming," he writes, "something like an inversion of attitude takes place. The very features of the sport which the 'C' swimmer finds unpleasant, the top-level swimmer enjoys. What others see as boring – swimming back and forth over a black line for two hours, say – they find peaceful, even meditative." This state of mind, which is the essential ingredient of flow, applies to individuals as well as teams. When people and teams take pleasure in working hard, they can enter a similar state of flow. And when outstanding companies are in flow, amazing outcomes that are often underappreciated by investors tend to result.

In summary, positive team dynamics is an important attribute of outstanding companies, as well as outstanding investment teams. A spirit of fairness and inclusion, effective feedback from leaders, and an attitude of continuous improvement are essential elements in the achievement of true excellence. Our goal at Victori Capital is to invest in extraordinary teams that exhibit these attributes, while pushing ourselves to the edge of our own abilities as investors, so that we, too, can reach beyond.

5 CULTURE

"The real voyage of discovery consists not in seeking new landscapes but in having new eyes."

Marcel Proust

While it is hard to define precisely, *culture* is often cited as a reason why companies, political parties, and countries struggle or thrive.

The notion of culture dates back to Socrates' times, when considerable thought was devoted to understanding how the Greeks differed from other civilizations. In the nineteenth century, as Charles Darwin and his contemporaries were taking special interest in the origins of human nature, the field of anthropology, which is essentially the science of culture, was born. One of the fathers of anthropology, Sir Edward Tyler, defined culture in page one of his seminal 1871 book, *Primitive Culture*, as "that complex whole which includes knowledge, belief, art, morals, law, custom, and any other capabilities and habits acquired by man as a member of society."[13] However, it was only in the 1980s that the methodical study of cultures began to be applied to the corporate world.

One of the pioneers in the field of organizational culture was Professor Edgar Schein, who defined it as "a pattern of shared tacit assumptions that was learned by a group as it solved its problems of external adaptation and internal integration, that has worked well enough to be considered valid and, therefore, to be taught to new members as the correct way to perceive, think, and feel in relation to those problems." Whereas the early anthropologists were more concerned with explaining why different cultures existed, Schein focused instead on why corporate cultures must be managed and changed. "There is no right or wrong culture," he wrote in *The Corporate Culture Survival Guide*, "no better or worse culture, except in relation to what the organization is trying to do and what the environment in which it operates allows."[14] Schein emphasized that some industries, technologies, and periods call for cultures that would fail miserably in a different setting or circumstance. "If you do not manage culture," he concluded, "it will manage you – and you may not even be aware of the extent to which this is happening." Jeff Bezos echoed this point in a 2008 interview with *U.S. News & World Report*: "Part of company culture is path-dependent – it's the lessons you learn along the way."

In her 2015 book, *The Silo Effect*, FT columnist and managing editor Gillian Tett discusses how cultures can form in destructive ways.[15] She highlights the role that silos play in forming cultural rigidities and offers strategies for combatting their dangers. Drawing from her Ph.D. in social anthropology and her experience as a journalist, Tett argues that the enduring success of any organization depends on the ability of its people to interact in ways that break down the debilitating silos which spring up over time. "The word 'silo' does not just refer to a physical structure or organization (such as a department)," she claims. "It can also be a state of mind. Silos exist in structures. But they exist in our minds and social groups, too. Silos breed tribalism. But they also go hand in hand with tunnel vision."

According to Tett, the financial crisis of 2008 was caused by mental silos regarding credit risk, as well as the organizational structures of financial institutions that promoted conflicting incentives and resulted in poor communication. She quotes Upton Sinclair in making her point about incentives: "It is very difficult to get a man to understand something when his salary depends on him not understanding it." One "silo-busting" strategy that Tett offers is for companies to tie compensation to overall performance, instead of the more common, "eat-what-you-kill" model. She also recommends that leaders promote a common purpose that transcends job descriptions.

The power of *purpose* in driving strong cultures and enduring success is also discussed in the book *Grit*, by University of Pennsylvania psychologist Angela Duckworth.[16] She writes, "Interest is one source of passion. Purpose – the intention to contribute to the well-being of others – is another." Duckworth evokes the parable of the bricklayers to make her case: "Three bricklayers are asked: 'What are you doing?' The first says, 'I am laying bricks.' The second says, 'I am building a church.' And the third says, 'I am building the house of God.' The first bricklayer has a job. The second has a career. The third has a calling." Duckworth concludes that when an organization's top-level goal is so consequential to the world that it compels all of its workers to see their job as their calling, formidable cultures emerge.

Duckworth also quotes from a study whereby journalist Studs Terkel interviewed hundreds of working adults in different professions and concluded that very few people view their work as a calling. "All of us," Terkel remarked, "are looking for daily meaning as well as daily bread...for a sort of life rather than a Monday through Friday sort of dying." Interestingly, those few people that Terkel found with a calling didn't always have professions that were conducive to purpose. They included seemingly mundane jobs like stonemasonry, bookbinding, and garbage collection. "I don't look down on my job in any way," one of his subjects was quoted as saying. "It's meaningful to society." Indeed, as Marcel Proust would say, purpose is in the eye of the beholder.

In summary, cultures are difficult to build and to maintain, but they are even harder to modify. Moreover, the most successful cultures are those that remain anchored to a common purpose that endures throughout the organization. This is why we pay close attention to not only the quality of the people in an organization, and the strategies that they deploy, but also how their culture changes through the good and the bad times. As former IBM Chairman Lou Gerstner put it, "Culture isn't just one aspect of the game – it is the game."

6   IMITATION

"Nature is commonplace. Imitation is more interesting."

Gertrude Stein

Imitation is often thought of as an undemanding, if not childish, form of behavior, but social scientists, biologists, and economists all agree on its importance to human intelligence and the development of culture, society, and markets. As investors in outstanding companies, we pay close attention to imitation and the various distortions that it can promote.

Imitation is not necessarily a bad thing. The benchmarking of best practices, for instance, is a widely accepted and benign form of imitation.

Politicians and countries imitate each other all the time, as do business leaders, athletes, and asset managers. Sometimes people imitate to gain an advantage, while other times they do it to promote empathy or to seek acceptance. It is when people imitate the wrong things unknowingly that the behavior becomes treacherous. In investing, even those who do not fall for mindless imitation remain exposed to that of others, especially when they take the form of investment fads and market bubbles.

Imitation has been widely observed in nature, from the lowest to the highest forms of animal life. In one study, female guppies, who have a genetic preference for bright orange males, were arranged to observe other females choosing dull-colored males, only to subsequently choose the dull males themselves. Like humans often do, the guppies overrode their instinct by choosing to imitate instead. In another well-known study, psychologist Solomon Asch put eight subjects in a room and asked them to identify two of four lines that were of equal length. While the answer was obvious, Asch instructed all but one member of each group to give the same wrong answer. The subjects were bright college students, yet one-third of them still went with the majority view. This study is often cited to illustrate how peer pressure, or groupthink, can result in poor decisions, as individuals succumb to irrational imitation.

Another less discussed drawback of imitation is that it tends to corrupt the quality of information we receive. In a book titled *News at Work – Imitation in an Age of Information Abundance*, Northwestern University Professor Pablo Boczkowski observes that the internet has not only changed how people consume news, but it has also enabled greater imitation among content creators, resulting in a decrease in the overall diversity and quality of the news.[17] The phenomenon can also be observed in Wall Street consensus estimates, where the forces of anchoring, clustering, and herding have increased due to improvements in information technology.

Haunted by the growing perils of imitation, how should a long-term investor in outstanding companies cope? We believe that McKinsey's book *Value – The Four Cornerstones of Corporate Finance* provides some credible answers.[18] Not surprisingly, the authors suggest that investors need to focus on the fundamental drivers of value, while accepting that prices will oscillate over shorter time periods. To illustrate their point, they propose a simplified model of the stock market, consisting of only two types of investors (A and B) trading a single company's stock. The A investors research the fundamentals and develop a view on the intrinsic value of the stock. They are non-imitators in the sense that they act on their own convictions. The B investors do not research the company, but instead, seek to imitate other investors by following the price trend. They buy on the way up and sell on the way down. Assuming the company's share price is below intrinsic value, the A investors will buy the stock until they drive the share price higher. The B investors, noticing the rising price, begin buying as well, thereby accelerating the upside move. As the price moves above the intrinsic value perceived by most A investors, they begin to sell, causing the stock to lose momentum and eventually decline. This induces the B investors to sell as well, causing the stock to decline further and faster. The cycle repeats unless evidence mounts that unexpected value has been created or destroyed. If a company announces a promising new product, for instance, the A investors might revise their estimate of intrinsic value higher and resume their buying. This, in turn, would trigger the beginning a new oscillation cycle around a higher price level. McKinsey's simple example illustrates two important points. The first is that share prices oscillate even when there is no new information. The second is that intrinsic investors ultimately drive the underlying levels at which share prices trade over time.

According to McKinsey, corporate finance theory is governed by only four timeless principles. The first is that a company's value is determined by its growth and its cash flow returns on capital. The second, to which they refer as the *conservation of value* principle, is that value can only be created by increasing future cash flows and not through financial engineering or other cosmetic means. The third principle relates to how the movement in stock prices reflect not only fundamentals, but changes in the market's expectations as well. This explains why great companies with bright futures don't necessarily make good investments if expectations are too high or deteriorating. The final principal is that the value of a business is not absolute but, rather, depends on who is managing it, and the strategy they pursue. By applying these core principles, they propose, investors can better guard against market distortions, while positioning themselves to benefit from long term-value creation.

In summary, imitation is widespread and its impacts can be both good and bad. As investors, we do not seek to avoid imitation altogether, but to remain on alert for the short-term volatility and irrational behaviors that it can spark. Finally, we aim to guard against these distortions by striving to remain independent thinkers, and by following the timeless laws of value creation.

7 FAILURE

"The opposite of failure is not safety. It's nothing."
Megan McArdle

Wikipedia defines failure as "the state or condition of not meeting a desirable or intended objective, and may be viewed as the opposite of success." Not meeting an intended objective is unquestionably a form of failure. But from the perspective of a long-term investor, failure is anything but the opposite of success. Rather, it is a core element of continuous improvement and risk mitigation. For an investor, the ability to fail well and fail fast explains successful outcomes better than the absence of failure itself.

Failing is natural, and its occurrence is widespread.

The very way that our brains develop is a showcase of failure. An infant's brain has twice as many synaptic connections as an adult's, making it more flexible and creative, as well as more capable of learning. But then children lose some 20 billion synapses per day between early childhood and adolescence. Through experience, certain connections get reinforced while others fail, resulting in a more efficient and coherent mind as the brain matures. This form of Darwinian selection, known as *synaptic pruning*, is an efficient way by which our neural circuits adapt to the demands imposed on them by the external environment. The process applies as well to brains as it does to industries, economies, and portfolios.

The similarities between brain development and industry innovation underscore a recurring concept in this book: that the workings of markets have strong parallels in nature. In *More than You Know*, Michael Mauboussin explores the analogy between brain development and economic progress.[19] He offers the evolution of the automobile, TV, disk drive, PC, and internet industries as vivid examples of the same pruning pattern that plays out in the child's brain as it matures. Investors allocate capital liberally in the early phases of growth, when the number of competing companies is large. But, as an industry matures, a process of rapid pruning takes place by which most companies get wiped out. As occurs in the brain of infants, the nascent industries become more efficient and more stable once they get clipped. Mauboussin argues that "investors are wise to look around for survivors at the end of a pruning process because a portfolio of surviving companies often presents an opportunity for attractive shareholder returns."

The parallels with synaptic pruning are also evident in risk management. When confronted with uncertainty, it helps to start with more alternatives before selecting the ones that are best suited to a given environment. Moreover, when the incidences of failure run low, the risks often rise until a new round of pruning takes place in the same iterative, Darwinian manner. In other words, a system that fails frequently tends to be more adaptive, making it better prepared to confront the next round of failures.

In *Dead Company Walking*, short seller Scott Fearon claims that "things go wrong more often than they go right," and that recognizing this was the single most important lesson he learned about business and life.[20] While many companies become better as a result of their failures and mistakes, others don't. Instead of avoiding the conditions that lead to permanent and catastrophic failures, Mr. Fearon seeks them out, and profits from their occurrence. He celebrates failure as "one of the most enduring and important American business traditions," and approaches it as fertile ground for exploiting human biases and generating profits.

Success, it would seem, requires learning how to fail well. Whether in parenting, education, or portfolio management, failing well means recognizing early the nature of mistakes. In his PhD dissertation about how doctors learn to avoid catastrophic mistakes, sociologist Charles Bosk proposed that there are essentially two types of errors: technical and normative.[21] The technical error is related to skill and judgment, and can generally be resolved through experience and practice. The normative error, however, is more serious because it involves an error of process and principle. An example of a normative error is when a pilot delays the recognition that he is lost, thereby putting more distance between his aircraft and the correct path. Another example is when an investor denies conflicting information so as to adhere to pre-existing beliefs. Normative errors are the reason why even minor disturbances, if not handled properly, can cascade into catastrophic failure.

A phenomenon that explains many incidences of catastrophic failure is known as *normalcy bias*. It is a cognitive state that people enter when facing a disaster, whereby they behave as if things are fine even when it is very clear that they are not. Like deer that freeze at a fast approaching headlight, people often die in wildfires, floods, and hurricanes when they fail to evacuate their homes as a result of this bias. Companies go bankrupt and investors get wiped out for this same reason: they do nothing when conditions call for action. The best way to protect against this bias is to be prepared for the worse. As the tagline of Mass Mutual Life Insurance company states: "You can't predict. You can prepare."

In summary, mistakes are normal, and failure is natural. The best companies are those that know how to fail frequently as they mature. The ability to deal well with failure is beneficial in many professional fields, as well as for life in general. Ultimately, it is those who can learn from repeated failures that reach the highest levels of success. As investors, we can achieve this by following a repeatable process, remaining prepared to fail, and accepting quickly our failures as opportunities to learn.

8 NARRATIVES

"The world is a story we tell ourselves about the world."

Vikram Chandra

Sometimes referred to as a story or a mental model, a *narrative* is often behind some of the most profitable decisions, as well as the most tragic mistakes, in history. Given their role in helping us make sense of a complex world, it is no exaggeration to say that life revolves around narratives.

People remember stories, yet the truth consists of hard, quantifying facts. While the influence of quantitative modeling has increased in the digital age, the notion of verifying narratives with facts and quantities is not new, though neither is it always possible. In the late 1800s, for instance, the accomplished physicist Lord Kelvin stressed the importance of constructing mechanical models to prove scientific theories. According to some accounts, Kelvin never accepted Maxwell's equations of electro-magnetism because he could not figure out how to construct mechanical models for them. A similar conflict exists to this day in the field of quantum mechanics, where the equations produce elegant solutions, but defy commonsense interpretation. Indeed, the physicists who ran with the numbers and eschewed interpretation came to be known as the "Shut up and Calculate" crowd. In financial markets these days, they are called *quants*.

While there would be tremendous advancement in the quantitative sciences during the dawn of the 20th century, it wasn't until 1943 that the philosopher Kenneth Kraik proposed the idea that the mind constructs small-scale models of reality that it uses to anticipate events. In his book *The Nature of Explanation*, which was written before computers were invented, Kraik likened the human nervous system to a calculating machine capable of modeling external events.[22] "If the organism carries a 'small-scale model' of external reality and of its own possible actions within its head," Kraik postulated, "it is able to try out various alternatives, conclude which is the best of them, react to future situations before they arise, utilize the knowledge of past events in dealing with the present and future, and in every way to react in a much fuller, safer, and more competent manner to the emergencies which face it." Kraik, who was just 29 when his book was published, but who died two years later in a bicycle accident, was clearly ahead of his time.

In his 2017 book *Narrative and Numbers*, NYU Finance professor Aswath Damodaran argues that the explosion in computing power and number crunching have ironically increased the demand for good storytelling.[23] He suggests that ubiquity of information, growth of social media, and the greater ability to multi-task, have actually made the current generation of investors less aware of the big picture than in the past. As a self-pronounced number-cruncher, Damodaran does not deny the power of a good story. He does warn, though, that when left unchecked, "stories can be extremely dangerous, not just for listeners but also the storytellers." To guard against the behavioral biases that good storytelling elicits, he recommends that a business narrative be grounded by believable facts and verifiable numbers. "When a storyteller has wandered into fantasyland," he writes, "the easiest way to bring him or her back to Earth is with data that suggests the journey is either impossible or improbable."

In assessing the merits of a business narrative, Damodaran also emphasizes the importance of the *corporate life cycle*, which he frames in six stages ranging from early growth to ultimate decline. "There is nothing more disconcerting in business," he asserts," than watching a narrator (who can be a founder, a top manager, or an equity research analyst) tell a story about a company that does not fit where that company falls in the life cycle: an expansive growth story for a company in decline or a story about sustainability for a young startup."

In his 2007 book *Doing What Matters*, James Kilts, who turned around Gillette before selling it to Proctor & Gamble in 2005, exposes the importance of getting the narrative right.[24] "Throughout my career," he writes, "I have considered both the content and the quality of my presentations – both external and internal – among my most important responsibilities, especially as a CEO." His book provides a wealth of guidance to managers, business owners, and investors alike. "Two of my lifelong mantras," he shares, "are *under-promise and overdeliver* and *say what you're going to do, only after you've done it.*"

Narratives matter not just to companies, but entire economies as well. In a recent paper titled *Narrative Economics*, Nobel Laureate Robert Shiller raises the question of whether the viral, or epidemic, spread of narratives can explain economic cycles.[25] He claims that economists have not paid enough attention to the propagation of such narratives during the most significant economic events in history. The first example he offers is that of the viral spread of the *Laffer Curve* narrative, which exploded into public attention in 1978, and became the main catalyst for tax cuts during the Reagan administration. Another example is that of the Great Depression, which he suggests was not necessarily caused by policy mistakes, but by the epidemic spread of a *morality* narrative that condemned wealth. "Sermons preached on the Sunday after the crash," he claims, "took great note of the crash, and attributed it to excesses, moral and spiritual. The sermons helped frame a narrative of a sort of day-of-judgment on the Roaring Twenties." Shiller's paper ends with an optimistic spin, as he concludes that the spread of a new "think big and live large" narrative in the U.S. might well boost consumption and entrepreneurial zeal.

In summary, investing can be just as much about storytelling as quantification. While narratives can help us in framing the truth, they can also lead us away from reality. The good news for long-term investors is that in time, the facts tend to prevail. "Great is the power of steady misrepresentation," wrote Charles Darwin in *Origin of Species*, "but the history of science shows how, fortunately, this power does not endure long."[26]

9   SIMPLICITY

"Innovation is saying no to a thousand things."

Steve Jobs

As investors in outstanding companies, we acknowledge the negative force that complexity exerts and how it tends to build over time. We aim to avoid a trend of growing complexity whenever we detect it and we look for great leaders who know how to fight the odds by keeping it simple.

Most successful companies start out simple but cannot avoid complexity as they grow the business. While technology and the network effect may produce economies of scale, most other factors do not scale as well. Employee interactions, customer focus, product development, and strategic vision are all common victims of complexity in larger organizations. Moreover, as leaders become further separated from the end customer, most companies struggle to remain simple.

Complexity inflicts not only organizations, but life in general. As the consultant Alan Siegel humorously points out in a recent book titled *Simple*, the United States was founded and governed for over two centuries on the basis of a single six-page document. Yet, these days, the income tax code alone runs over fourteen thousand pages. From utility bills and legal documents to insurance policies and medicine labels, it is hard to deny the growing challenge that complexity presents to our daily lives. [27]

The upshot of this widespread growth in complexity is that it places a greater premium on simplicity. Indeed, the offering of a simple solution within complex domains explains some of the greatest innovation successes in history. The challenge, though, is that accomplishing simplicity is not a simple matter. It requires an almost obsessive engagement from leaders, and a sort of focus that most big companies lack.

The power of simplicity is not a new idea. The Franciscan William of Ockham, best known for the *Ockham's razor* principle, was a prominent advocate in Medieval England. But the concept gained cult-like devotion in the Bauhaus design movement that emerged in Germany after World War I. The Bauhaus school reinforced simplicity, symmetry, and functionality, while downplaying unnecessary complexity. In a 1983 talk in Aspen, Steve Jobs publicly discussed his embrace of Bauhaus and how it would become the new "high tech." He was right. This same Bauhaus devotion to simplicity applies as equally to architectural design as it does to organizations and investing.

Just as simplicity can lead to greater customer and employee satisfaction, the lack of it tends to produce the opposite result in ways that are often unexpected. In a famous study from the field of social psychology, researchers from Columbia and Stanford Universities demonstrated how buyers of jams at a supermarket are six times more likely to purchase a jar when they are presented with six choices, than when they are presented with twenty-four.[28] "The desire to choose," they write, "often operates independently of any concrete benefit." Whereas classical economic theory relies on concepts of cost-benefit analysis to explain rational behavior, such research has shown definitively that the reality of choice follows a different set of rules. Basically, we all think we want more choices, but the more choices we get, the less satisfied and more confused we become. Some have referred to this phenomenon as *decision fatigue*, which is essentially another permutation of the same complexity that inflicts governments, companies, and investment portfolios alike.

Another domain where complexity has created havoc is investment management. In his 2014 book *The Investor's Paradox*, veteran fund-of-funds manager Brian Portnoy promotes the notion of success through simplification.[29] He claims that institutional investors today are overwhelmed by choices, brought about by the convergence of mutual funds, hedge funds, ETFs, as well as the explosion in the availability of information. The solution is focus. His company picks its managers based on only four core criteria: trust, risk, skill, and fit. According to Portnoy, method matters more than content, and endless information gathering without a method to structure it, is like drinking from an inexhaustible firehose.

With the goal of making systematically rigorous decisions, we strive for simplicity at Victori Capital, both in form and function. While the simple answers are not always easy to arrive at, we've come to appreciate that it's often those few simple decisions that make the greatest difference.

10   COMMON SENSE

"Common sense is what tells us the earth is flat."

Stuart Chase

Wikipedia defines *common sense* as "a basic ability to perceive, understand, and judge things, which is shared by nearly all people." While common sense is widely accepted as a prerequisite to successful investing, to the extent that it is shared by most people, it is unlikely to produce superior results. In investing, outstanding results can only be achieved by true contrarians who apply a logic that is less common, yet more accurate, than what gets offered up as common sense.

As the quote above implies, common sense is not always good sense, even though it is essential to the functioning of everyday life. In his provocative book *Everything is Obvious: Once You Know the Answer*, sociologist Duncan Watts warns of the dangers of relying too much on common sense.[30] "The paradox of common sense," he writes, "is that even as it helps us make sense of the world, it can actively undermine our ability to understand it." Watts observes that being critical of common sense can be tricky, because it involves the rejection of something that is universally regarded as a good thing. As he cynically asks: "When was the last time you were told not to use it?"

It has been said that common sense is the essence of social intelligence, as it is deeply embedded in our practical lives. Often, though, what we consider to be common sense is more influenced by individual and group biases than most of us realize. One example of these influences was researched by Güth, Schmittberger, and Schwarze in the 1980s, and became known as the *ultimatum game*. In this game, the first player (the proposer) receives a non-trivial sum of money (say $100) and proposes how to divide it with another player (the responder), who then chooses to accept or reject the proposal. If the proposal is accepted, both players keep their share, but, if it is rejected, both players take nothing. In hundreds of these experiments conducted in western industrialized societies, researchers demonstrated that most players propose a fifty-fifty split, and that offers below 30%

are typically rejected. Because it is common sense that fairness pays, responders typically prefer to punish an unfair offer than to take free money. But, when the experiment was reproduced with the Au and Gnau tribes of Papua New Guinea, the proposers consistently offered responders more than 50%, and surprisingly, these offers were often rejected. The Au and Gnau tribes, as it turned out, have strong customs about gift exchange, in which receiving a gift obligates the receiver to reciprocate. What might have seemed like a hyper-fair offer of free money to a Western participant looked like an unwanted obligation in Papua New Guinea. The moral of these findings is that an overreliance on common sense can inhibit our understanding of people's incentives and behaviors. This insight applies to the way we interpret world news, vote for our leaders, and select our stocks.

Market history provides ample evidence of how the notion of common sense changes with perspective. In *The Great Depression: A Diary*, Benjamin Roth recounts how he reacted to the historic events of the 1930s as they unfolded.[31] While the economic history books associate this difficult period with deflation, Roth was clearly obsessed with inflation instead. In fact, the word "inflation" appears 199 times in the book, while "deflation" appears only 5 times. Like many others of his time, Roth feared a repeat of the German hyperinflation scenario in the early 1920s, which he described as "a huge fraud which benefited the debtors and speculators at the expense of the large, prudent middle class." While these days it is considered common sense that the Fed should print money to fight deflation, this January 1936 diary entry highlights how times have changed: "I am personally very much concerned with the question of inflation and it seems to me there is a grave possibility it will come unless the government at once balances its budget. With an election coming, this seems out of the question." While Roth was an independent thinker, his fear of inflation kept him bearish on US Treasuries, which turned out to be the best asset class of his time. In other words, he was not really a contrarian on the subject of sound money.

So, what does being contrarian really mean? Forbes columnist Ken Fisher argues that it is not necessary for investors to do the opposite of consensus in order to be contrarians and to outperform the crowd.[32] If most people are bullish, for instance, a contrarian position might be even more bullish. The idea is that the direction of the consensus view can often be right, even when the magnitude is not. Contrarians do not have to confine themselves to buying low and selling high, and neither do they have to trade against the market. In fact, some of the best contrarian bets have the longest shelf lives. It is common sense, for instance, that stocks get more expensive when they go up. The reality, though, is that serial compounding can paint a much different picture. To paraphrase Howard Marks' comment from a talk we attended in 2015: "When you look at a stock that's gone up for 20 years and wish you had owned it, think of all the times, when it was making new highs, that you would have thought: maybe I should sell." The reality is that serial compounding often defies common sense.

To conclude, that which is common sense is not always right. It is also more important to be right than to be a contrarian. That said, the best profit opportunities exist when the right call is justified by uncommon views. At Victori Capital, we like to think of ourselves as long-term contrarians who look for repeatability and continuity where common sense might suggest otherwise.

11 TIME

"It takes a long time to bring the past up to the present."

Franklin D. Roosevelt

The notion of time has played a central role in finance since the Middle Ages, when the concept of discounted cash flows was introduced in Europe by the mathematician Leonardo Fibonacci. From the very first long-term government bonds that were issued in medieval Italy, to the most complex derivatives of the present, the passing of time has remained of paramount importance to the capitalization of investment returns. As such, coping poorly with time, or worse yet, misunderstanding its constraints, explains some of the biggest mistakes not only in investing, but in life generally.

In his recent book *Why Time Flies*, New Yorker staff writer Alan Burdick explores the perception of time by humans as well as less sophisticated animals.[33] He explains how rats, birds, rabbits, and even fish can perform uncanny feats in timing. In one of the studies that he cites, biologists at the University of Edinburgh demonstrated how hummingbirds in the wild could determine the flower-shaped sweetened water feeders with the highest refill rates and do so with impressive precision. "It seems like a sophisticated behavior," he writes, "but clearly it's fundamental to the animal kingdom, and the fact that it can be done by creatures with brains no larger than peas strongly suggests that there's some sort of timing device in there, one that is both basic and ancient." While the book focuses on our innate ability to sense and cope with shorter periods of time, such as this very instant or a moment ago, it also explores how easily our cognition of time durations can be influenced by our surroundings. "The perception of time is contagious," Burdick contends. "As we converse with and consider one another, we step in and out of one another's experience, including other's perceptions (or what we imagine to be another's perception, based on our own experience) of duration." The implication is that our perception of time is not entirely within our control, and awareness of its variations is not entirely effortless.

The impatience of others, for example, can make us less patient, too, without us even realizing it. As Warren Buffett frequently reminds us, "successful investing takes time, discipline, and patience."

The passing of time is no illusion, but the human mind still struggles with it. In a 2013 paper titled *The End of History Illusion*, researchers Jordi Quoibach, Daniel Gilbert, and Timothy Wilson demonstrated that people tend to misjudge how their preferences and values will change over time.[34] "Time is a powerful force that transforms people's preferences, reshapes their values, and alters their personalities," they write, "and we suspect that people generally underestimate the magnitude of those changes." After surveying 19,000 subjects aged 18 to 68, the authors conclude that most people under-appreciate how much they will change going forward, no matter their age. The paper ends with the paradoxical assertion that, in our minds, "history seems to always be ending today." Likewise, as the Roosevelt quote implies, history tends to take its time in reaching the present. Such illusions explain why people often fail to adequately save for retirement. It is also the reason why continuous improvement is so often underappreciated, or why serial compounding can remain mispriced for long stretches of time.

That markets struggle with time horizons is nothing new. In 1937, John Maynard Keynes complained that investors "are concerned, not with what an investment is really worth to a man who buys it 'for keeps', but with what the market will value it at, under the influence of mass psychology, three months or a year hence." Keynes' criticism seems even more justified today than it did in the 1930s. However, as the Schumpeter column in the February 18, 2017 issue of *The Economist* argued, these "supposedly myopic markets" that people complain about, in fact, look far into the future. "Amazon is the world's fifth-most valuable firm," the article points out, "with a colossal $400bn market capitalization. About 75% of that value is justified by profits that are expected to be made a decade or more from now. It is probably the biggest bet in history on a company's long-term prospects." Indeed, the *end of history* has no part in the Amazon narrative.

In *The Marshmallow Test*, psychologist Walter Mischel argues our minds have a *hot* system that compels us to react immediately to stress, even when it isn't in our best interest.[35] "This response," he explains, "was adaptive in evolutionary history for dealing with oncoming lions because it produces amazingly rapid (in milliseconds), automatic, self-protective reactions, and it is useful in many emergencies in which survival requires instant action. But this *hot* response is not useful when success in a given situation depends on staying cool, planning ahead, and problem-solving rationally." Mischel's advises us to constantly force our minds to imagine ourselves in the future as a means of improving decision-making. "To resist a temptation, we have to cool it, distance it from the self, and make it abstract. To take the future into account, we have to heat it, make it imminent and vivid. To plan for the future, it helps to pre-live it at least briefly, to imagine the alternative possible scenarios as if they were unfolding in the present. This allows us to participate in the consequences of our choices, letting ourselves both feel hot and think cool." Since the past is the best guide as to what might happen in the future, replaying past events, such as a bad year or decade, as if they were happening to us in the present, is also a useful and informative technique.

In summary, time is as difficult to understand as it is to resist. The magnitudes of change that time fosters, however, makes it worthy of the effort. Indeed, this is the essence of investing, and the reason we study our companies over such long time spans, while contemplating their prospects under a multitude of plausible futures. As investors in outstanding companies, the time we spend ensuring that time is indeed on our side, is time well spent.

PART II

MARKETS

THE OUTSTANDING FACTOR

12 POWER LAW

*"To improve at chess, you should in the first
instance study the endgame."*

José Raúl Capablanca

As per *Wikipedia*, "a power law is a functional
relationship between two quantities, where one
quantity varies as a power of another." While
many phenomena, such as the height or the
cholesterol readings for a particular population,
tend to follow a normal distribution (where values
have a central tendency), other phenomena, such as
the value of companies in a market, tend to follow
a power law distribution (where a few players
represent the majority of the aggregate value).
People are generally conditioned to reason in terms
of normal distributions, so they miss the way that

stock prices change over time in a power law world. Instead of aggregating around a stable mean, small differences in compounding rates, when sustained for long enough, make it such that a handful of companies will radically outperform all others.

The early 1900s Italian economist Vilfredo Pareto discovered what would become known as the *Pareto principle*, or the 80-20 rule, which is a power law function. Pareto's insights have found application across many disciplines, including business, biology, geology, and sports. Pareto observed that 80% of the wealth of countries was owned by 20% of the population, just as 80% of the peas from his garden came from 20% of the peapods. Likewise, the most destructive earthquakes are many times more powerful than all smaller ones combined, and the majority of tournaments are won by a few formidable players. Indeed, the phenomenon applies neatly to the market, as some 80% of the total value is concentrated in the top 20% of stocks.

As we have stated before, at Victori Capital we strive to find the few outstanding companies that can deliver outsized returns over longer time periods than is typically appreciated. The reason we believe these opportunities exist is that investors and managers are anchored to short-term fluctuations and conditioned to think in terms of simple averages. This causes them to lose sight of the endgame. Instead of outcomes that are normally distributed, the power law principle dictates that only a few companies will attain exponentially greater value in the future than all others combined.

In his book *Zero to One*, Peter Thiel describes the importance of power law thinking to venture capital investing.[36] He claims that any investor who over-emphasizes diversification instead of a single-minded pursuit for the very few companies that can become overwhelmingly valuable, will likely miss those rare companies in the first place. While running a diversified portfolio has its merits, Thiel also claims that investors who understand the power law principle make as few investments as possible, so that they can concentrate on the special candidates, just as a company would do when selecting a CEO or an individual would do when finding a spouse. Because time and decision-making themselves follow a power law, Thiel promotes the notion of focusing our efforts on higher impact decisions. He explains that, while young venture capital portfolios show little divergence in returns, a mature fund is typically split between one dominant investment and everything else. "Most of the differences that investors and entrepreneurs perceive every day," he writes, "are between relative levels of success, not between exponential dominance and failure."

The challenge is that, in a world that denies power laws, what's most important is rarely obvious.

Unlike with start-up investing or CEO selection, where trading liquidity is structurally constrained, the ability of investors to trade common stocks at will makes it harder for them to benefit from the power law principle. This is because, even when they select the right stocks, most investors over-trade, and thereby miss out on the opportunity to gain from the exponential dominance that emerges only over time. There is no lack of advice from the likes of Warren Buffett, who preach that investors should turn off their quote machines and focus on long-term fundamentals, but all too often, deep-rooted psychological biases still get the upper hand. The most prominent of these biases is loss aversion, which often manifests itself through myopic thinking.

Psychological influences represent a formidable challenge to not only investors, but most competitive endeavors. In *The Art of Learning*, chess player Josh Waitzkin, who was made famous by the movie *Searching for Bobby Fisher*, as well as his impressive achievements in competitive martial arts, claims that most of his defeats were not due to lack of skill, but psychological influences.[37] Josh's secret to coping with the inevitable psychological pressures of high-level competition is to stay intensely focused on the endgame from the beginning, and to suppress reactive thinking. As the quote by José Raúl Capablanca suggests, there is no better time to focus on the endgame than in the first instance.

In summary, we are not constrained by averages. We appreciate the 80-20 rule, and are intent on selecting only those stocks that stand a good chance of separating themselves from the pack over time. Finally, we aim to stay focused on the fundamentals, while avoiding the tendency to trade around short-term moves, and suppressing the urge to react to the noise that invariably comes with new information.

13 PATH DEPENDENCY

"True life is lived when tiny changes occur."

Leo Tolstoy

The concept of path dependence is prominent in both the natural and the social sciences, and it helps to explain many of the distortions, inefficiencies, and opportunities observable in otherwise efficient markets. Path dependence is also central to explaining why the future is so hard to predict. As Tolstoy's quote above suggests, an important implication of path dependence is that large, readily observable outcomes are explained by many small changes that receive less attention.

Leo Tolstoy was a realist who proposed a view that recorded history is misleading in that it "presents only a blank succession of unexplained events." Tolstoy believed that real history is created in the trenches, at the micro level, where human interactions occur and millions of decisions are made. Tolstoy's theory applies neatly to stock selection. While the media focuses on the big news, the greatness of companies is often achieved through the repeatable deployment of small advantages. This philosophy is central to our investment approach.

A classical depiction of path dependence was offered by the Hungarian mathematician George Pólya in the early 1900s. In the most basic Pólya urn model, the urn starts out with one white and one black ball. One of the balls is then drawn randomly and is returned to the urn together with an additional ball of its same color. This procedure is performed repeatedly and the ratio of black to white balls is observed. As with markets and economies, the ultimate ratio cannot be known ahead of time, and multiple trials yield vastly different results. Importantly though, the flexibility of the outcomes decreases rapidly, because once a black ball is drawn, for instance, the probability that another black ball gets drawn increases sharply. After a few successive, and increasingly likely, draws of black balls, it becomes nearly impossible for white balls to dominate. Positive feedback mechanisms, such as those portrayed by matching colored balls, are the drivers of path dependence. They help to explain why industries tip in favor of certain products early on, why markets are prone to extreme outcomes, why the rich get richer, and why viruses spread.

Another distinct, yet closely related, concept in path dependence is known as imprinting, which describes how initial environmental conditions leave a persistent imprint on organizations and societies, resulting in biased outcomes and behaviors long after the environment changes. In an informative and thought-provoking book titled *Reinventing American Healthcare*, Ezekiel Emanuel offers a contemporary example of this phenomenon at work[38]. He claims that: "The American health care system was not created complex and ridiculously expensive from its origins. It evolved to become this way over a period of about 100 years. And there is nothing inherent in the way it evolved. It could have been different. But many decisions, often made for reasons having nothing to do with improving health care, shaped the health care system we have today."

Emanuel evokes path dependence not only to explain the present, but also to boldly predict the future of American health care. He points out that it is important to focus on the history of reform, because the last battle sets the stage for future war and previous failed efforts have shaped subsequent attempts to reform. Using this framework, he foresees, among other notable outcomes, the end of employer-sponsored health insurance and of health care inflation over the next decade. But if the Pólya urn model teaches us anything, there is a high likelihood that he will be revising his predictions as alternative paths emerge and new imprints are made.

In summary, we are big believers in the influence that path dependence has on markets and other social systems, such as companies and governments. While we are aware of the random nature of complex systems and are careful not to place too much emphasis on causation, we are students of history and believe that being so improves our ability to make sense of reality, select stocks, and manage risk. Importantly though, because our focus is on finding outstanding companies with prospects that are under-appreciated in the market, we borrow from Tolstoy in emphasizing the significance of the tiny changes that persist over time.

14   MEAN REVERSION

"Fortune makes a fool of those she favors too much."

Horace

Mean reversion may be defined as a statistical phenomenon where the greater the deviation of an outcome from its mean, the greater the probability that the next measured outcome will deviate less. Just as stock prices and valuation multiples appear to frequently mean-revert from extremes, so too do the performances of companies, investors, and athletes.   Such oscillations can complicate the detection of underlying trends or create the appearance of trends where none exist.

The classic coin-flip experiment illustrates how a

phenomenon as simple and commonplace as mean reversion can warp our interpretation of reality. We know from theory that the probability of correctly guessing the result of a fair coin toss is always 50%, since each toss is independent of the one that preceded it. Indeed, if we were to toss a coin one million times, the odds of getting close to half heads and half tails are very high. What is not so obvious is how uneven the build-up of outcomes can become along the way. There is a relatively high probability, for instance, that the first one hundred tosses will produce a result that is quite different from 50/50. Knowing that the outcomes must revert to the mean over time does not help one determine when and how that will happen. In fact, one can never develop an edge in coin flipping, no matter how likely it might appear that either heads or tails are due to catch up. This illusion of statistical outcomes eventually catching up, as if "being due a break," is so common in casinos that statisticians have named it the *gambler's fallacy*.

When both skill and luck play a role in determining outcomes, the interpretation of mean reversion becomes more complicated than with coin flipping. Lucky streaks, for instance, can inspire confidence instead of skepticism, and an urge to press on rather than bet the other way. In his book *The Success Equation*, Michael Mauboussin writes that, "reversion to the mean is a trap that ensnares a lot of people, from individual investors buying a hot mutual fund to learned economists who misinterpret their findings."[39]   According to him, mean reversion creates three distinct illusions. The first is an illusion of cause and effect, or the inclination to look for what is causing a given measure to revert to the mean. The second is an illusion of feedback, where it appears that otherwise random outcomes are path dependent. The third and most subtle is an illusion of declining variance, or the idea that everything we can measure converges to a common value over time.

Mauboussin also points out that in complex systems such as markets, that are path dependent and follow a power law, mean reversion can lose relevance over time. This occurs because mean reverting noise tends to cancel itself out while the repeatable, underlying trends prevail.   Indeed, even small, yet persistent, advantages can allow a winner to take an increasing share of rewards, while remaining largely unnoticed.   This is the essence of serial compounding.

In *Full House: The Spread of Excellence from Plato to Darwin*, Stephen Jay Gould argues that trends must not be considered in isolation, but rather against the full range of their variations over time.[40] He challenges mainstream theory by arguing that "evolution rarely proceeds by the transformation of a single population from one state to the next. Such an evolutionary style, technically called *anagenesis*, would permit a ladder, a chain, or some similar metaphor of linearity to serve as a proper icon of change. Instead, evolution proceeds by an elaborate and complex series of branching events, or episodes of specification (technically called *cladogenesis*, or branch-making)." He offers the modern horse as a classic example of how evolutionary trends get misinterpreted by this bias of linear thinking. "The lineage of *Hyracotherium* to *Equus*," he writes, "represents only one pathway through a very elaborate bush of evolution that waxed and waned in a remarkably complex pattern through the last 55 million years. This particular pathway cannot be interpreted as a summary of the bush; or as an epitome of the larger story; or, in any legitimate sense, as a central tendency in equine evolution. *Equus* is the only living genus of horses, and therefore the only *modern* animal that can serve as an endpoint for a series." The daunting conclusion from his book is that even when trends do exist, they often can't be trusted.

Even those who choose to downplay the importance of mean reversion are unlikely to escape from its impact. For example, a wide body of research has shown that very few firms have sustained superior economic performance for long. Some even argue that technology is resulting in an accelerated pace of reversion to corporate mediocrity. To quote Jeremy Grantham, cofounder of GMO: "Profit margins are probably the most mean-reverting series in finance, and if profit margins do not mean-revert, then something has gone badly wrong with capitalism."[41] History leaves little doubt that aggregate profits tend to mean revert, but it also demonstrates that a company capable of sustaining superior returns for longer than expected can represent a tremendous risk/return proposition.

In summary, mean reversion is a fact of life, and a force to be reckoned with. As such, when it comes to outstanding companies, the question of sustainability cannot be taken lightly. Central tendencies can be useful in identifying and tracking underlying trends, but they are insufficient at best, and more likely to be misleading when dealing with complex systems. While nothing lasts forever and trees don't grow to the sky, persistence can be precious, not just in markets and sports, but in life generally.

15 CONTAGIOUSNESS

"The difficulty lies not so much in developing new ideas as in escaping from old ones."

John Maynard Keynes

As investors, we are constantly confronted with new ideas, both good and bad. Some catch on while others dwindle, but, as the quote above suggests, escaping the bad ideas is often more important, and more difficult, than coming up with promising ones.

In his 1976 book *The Selfish Gene*, evolutionary biologist Richard Dawkins proposes that certain ideas, beliefs, and cultures are like genes in that their replication is subject to a Darwinian process of natural selection.[42] Dawkins coined the term *meme* to describe such ideas, because they can be thought of as being related to 'memory'. "Memes," he writes, "should be regarded as living structures, not just metaphorically, but technically. When you plant a fertile meme in my mind you literally parasitize my brain, turning it into a vehicle for the meme's propagation in just the way that a virus may parasitize the genetic mechanism of a host cell." A notable attribute of *memetics*, as the theory has come to be known, is that it sidesteps the traditional concern with the truth of an idea, and focuses instead on its success at replicating. The implication is that bad ideas, from no-doc subprime mortgages to cigarette smoking, can be just as contagious as good ones.

Even though bad ideas can spread to a dangerous extent, the process of natural selection does a good job of eventually weeding them out. Evolutionary theory postulates that the most successful ideas are those that can thrive in an environment where they ultimately dominate. This attribute, known among game theorists as an evolutionarily stable strategy (ESS), explains why good ideas like cooperation ultimately prevail in an otherwise selfish world. Exploitative strategies can spread for a while, but they ultimately perish because they run out of unsuspecting hosts. This is the reason why deadly viruses don't survive, and why bad ideas that initially thrive are doomed to fail.

In the book *Contagious*, Jonah Berger proposes several principles that explain why a few ideas, products, or concepts go viral while most others don't.[43] As with memetics, he focuses on the attributes of an idea that drive replication and propagation, instead of the quality of the ideas themselves. The first and most relevant of his six principles is that contagious ideas must carry *social currency* in order to propagate through word of mouth. When a YouTube clip or a rumor makes people who share it look smart or plugged-in, it is said to contain social currency. Just as people use money to buy things, they use social currency to achieve a desired impression on others. To illustrate his thesis, Berger gives the example of a restaurant in Philadelphia called Barclay Prime, which became famous for its one-hundred-dollar cheesesteak. Paying so much for a sandwich may qualify as a bad idea to some, yet, according to Berger, "people didn't just try the sandwich, they rushed to tell others." The fact that the sandwich became a sensation was less about its ingredients and taste, and more about the story that its price tag inspired. Had the same sandwich been priced more reasonably, for instance, there would have likely been nothing remarkable to talk about.

The notion of social currency is quite relevant in stock selection, since few things provide more social currency to an investor than owning a stock that goes up a lot. Whether they hold onto winners for too long or sell out of them too soon, social currency has a wicked way of corrupting sound investment decisions. With the advent of the internet and the spread of social media, the impact of social currency on investing is likely to be intensifying. Perhaps more than ever, an appealing investment theme or story can become more popular than its fundamentals would justify. But, then again, so too is the process of natural selection, and its ability to weed out the bad ideas.

In summary, there is no lack of ideas, good and bad. Moreover, the propensity of an idea to spread rapidly does not necessarily make it a good idea. As investors, it is imperative that we understand not only the inherent merits of ideas, but also why and how they spread. In particular, we must stay alert to the tendency of seemingly good ideas self-destructing once they've spread too far. Especially for long term investors, the best ideas are the ones based on sound economics that endure.

16 CAUSALITY

*"Good tests kill flawed theories; we remain alive
to guess again."*

Karl Popper

The Oxford dictionary broadly defines causality as
"the principle that everything has a cause." Market
commentary during earnings season is a good
example of this theory being put to practice, as
stock price changes invariably get explained by the
news of the day, even when it doesn't justify the
move. Companies often beat earnings and raise
guidance, for example, only to watch their stocks
trade lower, as the media scrambles to explain the
nature of the disappointment.

While connecting the dots can be an effective way

to reach investment decisions, we must guard against the danger of confusing correlation with causation. As Tyler Vigen humorously highlights on his website, spurious correlations are plentiful, and include examples such as a 99.26% correlation between the per capita consumption of margarine and the divorce rate in Maine over the past decade. Another curious example of data mining was provided by David Leinweber, who showed that there was a 75% correlation between butter production in Bangladesh and the level of the S&P 500 from 1981 to 1993.

In *Thinking, Fast and Slow*, Daniel Kahneman proposes that much of what goes on in our minds when we associate cause with effect is completely alien to our experience.[44] "It is true," he writes, "that you know far less about yourself than you feel you do." His thesis on what really draws humans to their convictions has important implications for investors, because it highlights how often our views and decisions are influenced by biases that we cannot experience, much less control. The key conclusion from Kahneman's book is that when causality is at play, it is far better to think slow and think twice. Likewise, his work confirms the importance of testing our convictions with empirical evidence in order to avoid the causality trap.

While a deliberate attempt to test ideas with

empirical evidence may contribute to more robust decisions, it isn't a silver bullet when it comes to complex domains such as the stock market. The problem is that not everything that matters can be measured, and many of the things that can be measured simply do not matter. Another problem is that regardless of how much data one samples, a hypothesis or theory can never be definitively proven, and remains at all times immediately falsifiable. Better known these days as *Black Swan Theory*, this unresolved asymmetry in the theory of knowledge has been a subject of debate for centuries. It did not matter, for example, that the Old World had sampled millions of white swans before the discovery of Australia; all it took was the appearance of a single black swan in the land down under to shatter the universal theory that all swans are white. As Nassim Taleb has pointed out, "the discovery of black swans illustrates a severe limitation of our learning from observations or experience and the fragility of our knowledge." [45]

In spite of all the controversy, there is no denying that practical knowledge, of the kind that supports robust decision making, must be grounded in sound theory. In his book *The Innovator's Solution*, Clay Christensen provides a framework for theory building that we have found useful in our pursuit of outstanding companies.[46] According to his view, it is bad categorization, not bad causality, which often leads to unreliable theories. If investors or managers attempt to extrapolate successful choices from prior experience without taking the differences in circumstance into account, the results are often poor. Many management books fall prey to this trap: they draw from common attributes across multiple organizations and time periods before offering them as general prescriptions for how to build a winning organization. With this approach, they miss the notion that the strategies that worked well for one company or industry in the past may not be the best prescription for running another company in a particular industry today.

The randomness of markets, the limitations of empirical learning, and the difficulty of theory building, present formidable challenges to investors. With this in mind, we deploy an investment process that is founded on sound theory. We are aware that unlike in most physical tasks, where skill and result are better correlated, the feedback loop in investing can be rather weak. In baseball, for instance, the players who work diligently at improving their batting skills can often drive up their batting averages. With investing, though, randomness often plays a bigger role in determining short-term success. Good decisions often feel like mistakes, while poor ones get rewarded by chance. Coping with randomness can be challenging, but we believe that, over time, the noise invariably cancels itself out, allowing the best processes to come out ahead.

In summary, establishing causality isn't easy, nor is it always desirable. While robust decisions demand sound theories based on empirical evidence, it is not always possible for the investor to determine what constitutes a mistake versus merely bad luck. The ability to learn from mistakes, while precious in investing, cannot be deployed without careful consideration of the circumstances. Finally, the best way to cope with the false signals that the market so often sends is to stay focused on process, while downplaying the implications of short-term results.

17 RADICAL UNCERTAINTY

"It is better to be roughly right than precisely wrong."

John Maynard Kaynes

The concept of radical uncertainty refers to relevant information that escapes detection and does not lend itself to any form of statistical analysis. It is the class of uncertainty that former US Secretary of Defense, Donald Rumsfeld, famously described in a televised response to a CNN reporter's question in February 2002 about the lack of concrete evidence surrounding Iraq's possessions of weapons of mass destruction. "There are known knowns; there are things we know we know. We also know there are known unknowns; that is to say we know there are some things we do not know. But there are also unknown unknowns — the ones we don't know we don't know."

While often neglected in politics, the concept of radical uncertainty is not new to economics. In a 1921 book titled *Risk, Uncertainty and Profit*, Frank Knight, who was Milton Friedman's professor and one of the founders of the Chicago school, described it as an uncertainty that "must be taken in a sense radically distinct from the familiar notion of risk, from which it has never been properly separated."[47] The type of risk he described would later become known as Knightian uncertainty, which Wikipedia defines as "risk that is immeasurable, not possible to calculate." John Maynard Keynes would come to agree with Knight that there exists a category of risk, which he called "uncertain knowledge," that has "no scientific basis on which to form any calculable probability whatsoever." Then in 2007, Nassim Taleb coined the term *black swan* to describe essentially the same phenomenon.

Whether in economics or philosophy, the need to deal with "unknown unknowns" represents a formidable challenge. The bottom line is that the complexity of not just markets, but life generally, far exceeds our capacity to understand everything that matters, let alone what has yet to matter. Faced with such a precariously uncertain reality, investors must find a way to cope.

In his 2016 book, *The End of Alchemy*, NYU Professor and former head of the Bank of England, Lord Mervyn King, proposes the adoption of simple coping strategies to handle the radical uncertainty phenomenon.[48] Whereas behavioral economists warn against an over-reliance on heuristics (i.e. rules of thumb), Lord King advocates their use for dealing with challenging tasks such as banking, investing, and government intervention. King gives the example of JP Morgan's CEO in the 1990s, Sir Dennis Weatherstone, who swore by a heuristic that would have avoided a lot of trouble in 2008. He simply did not approve new financial products he could not understand. "Investment has to be rational," he used to say. "If you can't understand it, don't do it."

Lord King was not the first to propose simple ground rules for coping with highly complex systems. Nobel Laureate Herbert Simon, whom some consider the father of artificial intelligence, introduced the notion of *satisficing* in 1947[49]. Simon's theory broke with the more traditional view of how economic agents behave. He showed how, in practice, decision-makers are not well-informed agents that follow rational choice theory. Instead, they make decisions under circumstances in which an optimal solution cannot be determined, and they seek to compromise more than they optimize. "Decision-makers can satisfice either by finding optimum solutions for a simplified world," he observed, "or by finding satisfactory solutions for a more realistic world." Simon concluded that, for natural problems, where information is lacking and explanatory formulas are intractable, mathematical optimization procedures simply do not apply. In other words, you cannot model a black swan.

Some have argued that just because human nature is hard to model does not mean we should not try. In an influential 1953 essay called *The Methodology of Positive Economics*, Milton Friedman argued that one should not evaluate a theory based on the validity of its assumptions, but, instead, on the accuracy of its predictions. He observed that, if billiards players who do not understand Newtonian mechanics can still play as if they did, so too can economic agents invest as if they had full understanding of rational choice theory.[50] A generation of quant investors would evolve after Friedman's endorsement of the very sort of mathematical modeling that his mentor, Frank Knight, dismissed, but the controversy remains to this day. John Kay, for instance, who is a respected British economist and a Professor at the London School of Business, recently wrote in the *Financial Times* that "Friedman was wrong." He continues: "There are things we do not know because we cannot imagine them. If you had described your smartphone to Mr. Friedman in 1976 he would not have understood what you were talking about, far less been able to speculate intelligently on the probability that it would be invented or bought. ... There is a world of difference between low-probability events drawn from the tail of a known statistical distribution and extreme events that happen, but had not previously been imagined. And it is usually the latter that gives rise to crisis – and opportunities."

In summary, reality is hard to understand and coping with it is an even bigger challenge. This is why it pays to keep an open mind and to follow basic rules of thumb that make sense. Investing in solid businesses with underappreciated secular growth is one of our simple rules. Another is to focus on important knowables, such as management track record. Finally, we do not lose sight of the fact that the only way to benefit from an uncertain future is to endure.

18 COMPLEXITY

"Evolution is chaos with feedback."

Joseph Ford

Since our goal is to find companies that remain outstanding over time, we cannot overlook the risks that rapid change, disruption, turbulence, and obsolescence pose to our investment objectives. Like fashion, stocks come into, and go out of favor all the time as the backdrop evolves and new trends take over. It is our belief, though, that there exists a small subset of outliers that manage to thrive in the chaos, and get stronger over time, much like how organisms thrive in nature. These are the companies that we want to invest in.

In his ambitious book *The Misbehavior of Markets*, Benoit Mandelbrot proposes that markets, industries, and economies are governed by the same complex processes that govern the rest of nature.[51] According to him, these systems are better understood through the concepts of chaos theory than conventional, deterministic models. In a 1972 study, Mandelbrot showed how changes in the airflow speed over an airfoil closely resembled changes in stock market prices. Instead of clustering around a mean, "price swings are highly erratic, with the large ones numerous and clustered together." Just as stocks rise and fall in seemingly recurring, though unpredictable patterns, so too does the speed of air as it switches erratically from orderly into gusty, turbulent flow. Mandelbrot's wind tunnel experiments confirm our original point in unintended ways. Aeronautical engineers know that simple vortex generators, when attached to a wing's upper surface, will "trip" the airflow into turbulent mode before it has the chance to separate. In a sense, a wing's performance can be improved with a controlled dose of the very turbulence that it seeks to avoid. A similar analogy is found in medicine, where venom is used to cure viruses, or in thermodynamics, where greater entropy promotes stability. We contend that companies are no different. Their ability to thrive in the face of continuous change is a function of how they adapt to change before it is allowed to become disruptive. This ability to use chaos to promote order is the true essence of adaptability.

The idea of organizations thriving at the boundary of order and chaos is explored in a book by Dee Hock, the founder of Visa, titled *Birth of the Chaordic Age*.[52] Hock defines the word *chaordic* as "the behavior of any self-governing organism, organization or system which harmoniously blends characteristics of order and chaos." An avid and eclectic reader, Hock admits that his ideas and management philosophies were inspired by the theories of prominent scientists and academics on the nature of complex systems. "There is something about the nature of complex connectivity," he writes, "that allows spontaneous order to arise, and when it does, characteristics emerge that cannot be explained by knowledge of the parts." Enabled by the explosion of information and technological innovation, which Hock was early to see coming, he claims that "we are living on the knife's edge of one of those rare and momentous turning points in human history." In this *new age*, the command-and-control institutions that defined the Industrial Age will give way to a new type of enterprise that self-organizes in the face of paradox and conflict. While Hock stopped short of providing in his book a concise list of the attributes shared by chaordic organizations, we have used his concepts, as well as the theories of other thought leaders such as

Mandelbrot, to propose the top three attributes of such organizations.

The first of these attributes is simplicity. The nature and purpose of any organization must be simple and clear enough for every participant to understand and follow. Simplicity is powerful in that it reduces the distance between leaders, employees, and customers, which in turn promotes agility and adaptability.

The second attribute is optionality, a concept that refers not only to a company's current set of choices, but also its ability to network and explore new degrees of freedom. Unbound by paradigms, a chaordic organization rarely sets internal growth targets. Instead, they abide by broad, guiding principles that open new possibilities and lead the way to progress. The ability to be creative while remaining simple is uncommon, but new examples of such organizations continue to emerge, not only in the technology space, but also in healthcare, transportation, and retailing.

The third and final attribute is risk dispersion. By this we mean a company's ability to succeed by accepting frequent failures. This is an attribute often associated with companies that are organized into numerous, self-contained entities, where people are empowered to innovate. While most companies fear failure, the chaordic organization engages in self-organized, repeatable processes of trial and error, and uses their feedback to drive continuous improvement. This dynamic is the essence of Joseph Ford's quote at the top of this chapter.

As investors and risk managers, we are focused on companies and themes that not only endure, but also improve with time. We cannot avoid uncertainty, disruption, and turbulence, and neither do we wish to do so. It is turbulence itself that drives evolution.

19 DISLOCATIONS

"While markets appear to work in practice, we are not sure how they work in theory."

Maureen O'Hara

As stated previously, our primary objective as investors is to capture the serial compounding that outstanding companies deliver over time. In order to achieve this goal, we focus on long-term fundamentals while respecting and preparing for market risk. One of these risks is that the market, not unlike other complex systems, is prone to price dislocations that are hard to explain, impossible to predict, and unlikely to be avoided. While we don't wish to minimize the importance of any one dislocation versus another, we must accept that market dislocations are the norm, yet stocks of outstanding companies have been compounding wealth for decades, if not centuries.

Crowds have a bad reputation, and not just in the stock market. The speculator Bernard Baruch famously said: "Anyone taken as an individual is tolerably sensible and reasonable – as a member of a crowd, he at once becomes a blockhead." While positive feedback among crowd participants can result in unstable market conditions and lead to the sort of dislocations that we aim to guard against, the crowd itself is not always to blame, and neither is it all that stupid. In *The Wisdom of Crowds*, author James Surowiecki argues that crowds are actually quite smart.[53] "Under the right circumstances," he writes, "groups are remarkably intelligent, and are often smarter than the smartest people in them. Groups do not need to be dominated by exceptionally intelligent people in order to be smart. Even if most of the people within a group are not especially well-informed or rational, it can still reach a collectively wise decision."

A classic demonstration of group intelligence is the jelly-beans-in-the-jar experiment. When the University of Southern California professor Jack Treynor ran the experiment in his class with a jar that held 850 beans, the group estimate was 871, and only 1 out of 56 people in the class made a better guess. The group average was closer to the actual bean count than most of the students' guesses, every time. By running the experiment repeatedly, Treynor showed that, while few people typically do better than the group in any given run, there was no evidence that certain people consistently outperformed the group.

A vast body of academic and practical research has confirmed that crowds are most intelligent when they have diversity. While large groups can benefit when members learn from each other, too much communication and agreement among members can actually make the group as a whole less intelligent. When people have different ideas, strategies and views, the crowd makes better predictions, and the market functions more efficiently. There are times though, when diversity weakens, and the collective judgement of the crowd becomes lopsided, if not irrational. It is when too many market participants begin to use similar investment strategies that the market becomes most susceptible to dislocations. We saw this with the growing popularity and ultimate demise of quantitative investment strategies in the mid-2000s. While dislocations aren't fun, they are often precisely what the market needs in order to regain its diversity and re-establish order.

As with many other phenomena, the occurrence of price dislocations in stock markets has strong parallels in nature. In his insightful book titled *Critical Mass*, physicist Phillip Ball argues that, like a liquid that will suddenly turn to solid when its temperature falls just slightly below the freezing point, social systems also have critical points beyond which they abruptly change in response to small perturbations.[54] But unlike in nature, where these critical points are typically known, they tend to be invisible in otherwise well-functioning societies and markets. The key insight is that large-scale outcomes can occur as a result of the internal workings of the system and not from some external shock. The implication is that complex social systems like markets can be vulnerable in ways that are not necessarily visible, and much less knowable. Moreover, the existence of such invisible critical points and phase transitions makes it challenging for investors to learn from history, as cause and effect are not always clear or proportionate.

In summary, markets are smart, but they can also be volatile and prone to unpredictable dislocations. Over the long term though, the stock market is a very efficient system for assessing and rewarding the creators of value. As capital allocators and risk managers, our goal is to capture enough of the outsized value that outstanding companies create over time, while mitigating the risk of large losses by staying defensive and remaining skeptical, especially when confronted with evidence of declining diversity. We accept that there will be critical points and dislocations along the way, and we see this as much a reason for optimism as for caution, for without these risks there would be less opportunities.

20 ANTIFRAGILITY

"We made too many wrong mistakes."

Yogi Berra

A question we often get asked is if the investment environment is becoming more dangerous? There is no way of knowing the answer to such a question, but even if we knew, it is even harder to select a proper course of action. Not investing is always an alternative, but as Warren Buffett put it in his 2012 letter to shareholders: "The risks of being out [of the market] are huge compared to the risks of being in it."[55]

It has been said that experience brings with it the realization that the future is rarely bright, and that concerns about it rarely disappear. The crowd, perhaps because of itself, is almost always focused on some big risks, but how much people discuss an event is a bad indicator of the actual risk associated with that event. In fact, the more people talk about a risk, the more likely it becomes that the particular risk will be mitigated. We saw this with the debt ceiling crisis in 2011 and we may well see it again with the end of quantitative easing.

To further complicate matters, it is only after they get added to history that events become explainable. A much longer list of alternative histories that didn't happen rarely get the credit they deserve. Even a careful study of history can prove illusive for this very reason, because not every mistake gets punished, and some may even be rewarded. This is the essence of Yogi Berra's quote above - and another reason why we strive to focus on what is knowable instead of reacting to what is beyond our control.

Fear is the number one reason why people stay out of stocks just when it would have been the most rewarding to get in. With stocks making new highs or new lows, fear tends to run high, including the fear that fear itself might not be high enough. The Fed, the Middle East, Russia, deleveraging, deflation, inflation, currencies, and commodities are all on the list of reasons to sell. As we stack up the degree of all these fears against periods in the past when they also prevailed, we cannot help but conclude that not much has changed.

So back to the central question that opened this chapter. A casual read of the Economist or the Financial Times might suggest that danger is building globally to alarming levels. With this very feeling in our own guts, we remembered of a book by Nassim Taleb titled *AntiFragile: Things that Gain from Disorder* - which we credit with having kept us from getting out of stocks at prior "scary" junctures.[56] While not as enjoyable of a read as his other books, Taleb proposes a useful concept for understanding the nature of risk. From his vantage point, turbulence itself is a positive trait, and he provides some great examples of how that is actually the case in nature.

Taleb claims that when governments attempt to stabilize the system through monetary and fiscal intervention, they only serve to make it inherently unstable and more dangerous over time. He may turn out to be right about that call from any given level, but he has been wrong for extended periods during which volatility measures of all sorts have continued to decline.

Our view is that government intervention is nothing new, and neither is the cyclical rise and fall of volatility. Instead of a system made more fragile by attempts to contain it, we see a global market today that has sustained multiple shocks over the past decade, after which it has emerged ever more *anti-fragile*, and therefore, safer. Like a muscle that gets stronger with abuse, or an organism that gains immunity to a germ via continuous exposure, the market too can become more robust following multiple periods of extreme volatility. As we have seen since the 2008 crisis, and likewise, following the 1929 crash - the quality of the bull market that follows tends to be proportional to the degree of pain in the preceding bear. What Taleb claims as a key argument in his case for rising volatility, is precisely the theory that we use to refute his argument. It is very possible that the market's muscle is getting stronger.

To summarize, we do not agree with the naysayers who succumb to fear of the future as a reason to stay out of the equity market. The notion that crisis looms just ahead must be used carefully, in our opinion, when the goal is efficient long-term compounding. Yes, it is true that we cannot predict what all the bad news will bring - but that is always the case, and it is exactly why we try to stay focused on detecting evidence of more tangible factors that are known to build wealth, such as cash flow compounding, repeatable processes, strong leadership, a meritocratic culture, a record of continuous improvement, and secular growth.

21 IMPERMANENCE

"Nothing endures but change."

Heraclitus

Buddhism defines *impermanence* as "the notion that all of conditioned existence, without exception, is transient or in a constant state of flux." The Buddha taught that, because conditioned phenomena are impermanent, attachment to them becomes the cause for future suffering. His teachings are as enlightening to investing as they are for life in general.

The footprint of impermanence is prominent in the history of the S&P 500 index, which was originally formulated in 1957. Notably, four of the top ten S&P constituents in 2015 (Apple, Microsoft, Google, and Walmart) weren't even in existence then. At its inception, the index was dominated by oil producers, railroads, and utilities, while these days more than half of its weight is concentrated in technology, financials, and health care. The index continues to include about five hundred stocks, but over one thousand names were replaced over the years.

As devoted long-term investors in outstanding companies, we've come to recognize that any investment theme, no matter how compelling, will eventually weaken. Even when fundamentals don't deteriorate, a seemingly attractive investment can underperform simply by peaking in popularity. For this reason, we are not dogmatic about our pursuit of attractive attributes, but focus instead on how the companies we consider outstanding might change relative to expectations, and for how long our variant view might persist. While our focus is on longer term trends, we do not believe in staying wrong for long when change fails to go our way. That said, the ability to endure in the face of change is one of the key traits of an outstanding company.

In 1994, Wharton professor Jeremy Siegel published the best seller *Stocks for the Long Run*, which went on to become known as "the buy-and-hold bible," due to its empirically driven conclusion that stocks go up over time.[57] With the benefit of the dot-com bubble in hindsight, Siegel then published *The Future for Investors* in 2005, where he focused more on the notion of impermanence.[58] Like the Buddha, Professor Siegel emphasized that nothing lasts forever. But unlike the Buddha, who preached the acceptance of this impermanence as true wisdom, Siegel advocated sticking with a specific type of "tried and true" stock for the long term.

The ideal stock, according to Professor Siegel, is one that benefits from a strong brand name, products that don't change over time, high cash flow and dividend yields, and an earnings multiple that is not much higher than the market's. He offered Hershey's, Heinz, and Coca Cola as prime examples of the type of stocks an investor should hold for the long run. Ironically, Siegel called these stocks *Corporate El Dorados*, in honor of the mythical, lost city of gold that was never found.

We agree with the attractiveness of the attributes that Professor Siegel highlights, and while we do not assume anything to be permanent, we can see why they might persist. In the end, whether one likes to invest in established companies, emerging growth, or distressed situations, it is less about the attributes themselves, and more about how they change in time, and relative to expectations.

One of the most valuable concepts in *The Future for Investors* is what Professor Siegel called the 'Growth Trap'. He defines it as the fallacy of assuming that just because an industry or company is growing rapidly, it represents a good investment. To avoid falling for this trap, Professor Siegel recommends industries and companies that are less popular for their growth, or even those that have bad reputations, and for which expectations stay stubbornly low. An outstanding company in an improving industry that is still considered toxic has been, and should remain, a formula for outsized returns. Nursing homes, trucking, and utilities are examples of such industries. They are not generally perceived as great, but may contain formidable companies with repeatable and highly profitable growth models that benefit from underappreciated secular trends.

While out-of-favor industries can be fertile ground for finding value, we do not shy away from industries and companies that are in favor if we believe their ability to sustain outsized returns is still underappreciated. Such stocks are often perceived as expensive, putting them out of reach of most value investors, even when in reality they might be bargains. We believe investors are systematically biased towards thinking in short-term, linear increments, and so they often underestimate the value that outsized compounding delivers in time. Perhaps because of the popularity of the notion that strength can't last forever, the value of the strongest and most enduring trends is frequently underappreciated by investors.

In summary, because everything is impermanent, we must remain on alert and flexible in coping with the changes that the future has in store. We cannot choose this future, and neither is it in our interest to fight it as investors. While we strive to position ourselves to benefit from longer-term trends, we are neither oblivious to cycles nor to the teachings of the Buddha.

22   SECULAR GROWTH

"Even if you are on the right track, you'll get run over if you just sit there."

Will Rogers

As quality investors, we look for special companies that can compound returns at above market rates in spite of macroeconomic cycles.   To find such companies, we seek not only outstanding businesses with strong managements, but also industries in secular growth. By focusing on stocks that we feel comfortable holding through cycles, we believe that we can improve our ability to compound without taking outsized cyclical risk. This is what attracts us to stocks that benefit from enduring, secular, global themes like urbanization, automation, digitization, and connectivity.

One challenge that we face as investors is that, in practice, even secular trends can have a cyclical element. The outstanding industries of today are not the same as yesterday, and they will likely not be the same tomorrow. Autos, for instance, used to be a secular growth industry. Same for newspapers, airlines, PCs, telecom services, and many others that today are saturated or plagued with new challenges. With this truism as context, we must stay focused on how secular trends are changing, and why they might improve, fade, or even come back full circle.

The North American railroad industry is an example of how secular trends cycle back in time. After taking center stage during America's gilded age, railroad financing turned into a bubble in the late 1800s, leading to significant overbuilding. For nearly a century thereafter, the industry would face detrimental share loss to the motor vehicle while suffering from a decline in US manufacturing and crude oil output. Over the past decade, though, railroads have been benefitting from secular growth again, thanks to the shale oil and petrochemical renaissance, as well as truck-to-rail conversions.

A secular theme that has stood the test of time is urbanization. The UN estimates that the share of the world's population living in urban settings rose dramatically from 13% in 1900, to 29% in 1950, to

49% in 2005, and 54% in 2014. With urban headcount continuing to grow faster than the overall population, the demand for basic sanitation, fresh water, and pest control should continue to increase, particularly in emerging markets, and irrespective of market cycles. Among other needs, the shift towards urban life has also been associated with the explosion in incidences of heart disease and diabetes in parts of the world, driving growth in basic healthcare services.

Automation, which includes robotics and machine vision, is another secular trend where we see opportunity. Beyond the well-known plays in the space, there are companies taking capabilities to new levels, and at lower costs. These include highly specialized providers of services in areas where robotics is a critical enabler, such as in the production of oil from the deep-water reservoirs, or the detection of metal contaminants in food products. With marked advancements in sensor technology and cellular robotics already evident, it will not be long before ocean floors, farms, and even highways are populated with colonies of self-guided, working class vehicles capable of performing tasks better than humans.

Digitization, and its accelerated penetration into all areas of human life, is another attractive hunting ground for secular growth. While *Big Data* is a popular concept, many of the longer-term impacts from the explosion of data are still underappreciated.

Technological innovation is also exploding, but that could be both good and bad. For instance, creative destruction and the risk of obsolescence could make it tougher to play in the handset business. We believe the emphasis is already shifting away from infrastructure and technology towards the transformation of massive raw data into useful insight. Prominent examples include the use of location and browsing data for targeted marketing, as well as the use of information on population health patterns for reducing healthcare costs.

Another secular growth theme we like is how connectivity keeps driving efficiency gains in far corners of the globe. *The Digital Age*, co-authored by Google's former Chairman, Eric Schmidt, presents the case of Congolese fisherwomen today: "Whereas they used to bring their daily catch to the market and watch it spoil as the day progressed, now they keep it on the line, in the river, and wait for mobile phone calls from customers."[59] This simple advancement has reduced cost, improved food safety, and enabled more people to live off of fishing, thereby increasing food supply and overall quality of life in Congo, the fourth most populous country in Africa.

In conclusion, while the path of growth in the near term gets most of the attention, we find that the market often overlooks the enduring nature of secular growth, and the long-term compounding that it enables. By focusing on the outstanding companies that can benefit from secular trends, we aim to improve our chances of receiving outsized returns with less macro risk.

23 AGING

"If at first the idea is not absurd, then there is no hope for it."

Albert Einstein

While hardly a new investment theme, we believe that population aging still ranks among the most relevant secular growth trends today. From pharmaceutical consumption and hospital utilization, to entertainment and lifestyle products and services, a rapidly aging population will most certainly continue to create new opportunities for profits that are currently undiscovered or under-appreciated.

As Gregg Easterbrook points out in *The Atlantic*, current projections of ever-longer life spans assume no incredible medical discoveries, even though such advancements are indeed becoming reality.[60] Scientists at the Buck Institute, for instance, have been able to quintuple the life span of laboratory worms, while similar results have been reproduced globally. In 2013, Google started Calico, a biotech company whose main goal is to tackle the process of aging. We agree with Easterbrook that breakthroughs in anti-aging research are not a pie in the sky, and that the centennials may become the norm sooner than many expect. If aging could be retarded, or who knows, avoided all-together, then the results could be a seemingly absurd increase in productivity.

It is not news that people are living longer. In fact, the average human life span has doubled in less than a century. In Japan, for instance, the number of people above 85 is expected to grow by over 60% in twenty years, even as their overall population declines. In the US, the Census Bureau expects the population above 85 to go from about 6 million today to 19 million in 2050. On a global basis, the population aged above 85 is expected to double in 20 years, and that above 100 is expected to increase four-fold. While the research and media reports on demographic trends routinely highlight the negative social and economic implications of an aging population, we see reason for optimism. We do not dismiss the reality that older people have tended to be less productive and more prone to chronic diseases that require expensive care. However, we see exciting opportunities and many positive implications from mankind's ability to extend healthy lives, and we prefer to focus on these dynamics instead of merely fearing the headwinds.

Like most other predictions about the future, those concerning population trends have a spotty record. At the start of the nineteenth century, for instance, Reverend Thomas Malthus predicted that massive population growth would inevitably result in widespread famine, disease, and conflict. Some 200 years later, and in spite of a seven-fold increase in population in conjunction with dramatically higher standards of living, Malthusian predictions about the lack of natural and social resources to cope with population growth remain prominent. While challenges do exist, we are firm believers that human ingenuity will continue to prove the naysayers wrong.

One area in which ingenuity is likely to surprise is the cure and treatment of chronic diseases. In the 1950s, economists predicted that caring for polio patients would be economically ruinous, but then came the polio vaccine. Likewise, it was not too long ago that AIDS was expected to take the life of one in every five Americans, and this now seems unlikely to ever happen. Today, experts are predicting that as the incidence of Alzheimer's triples by 2050, the cost to society will exceed the current US defense budget. Maybe one day they will prove right, but we suspect the poor track record of such gloomy predictions will continue to be the norm.

In a recent book titled *The Upside of Aging*, author Paul Irving, who is Chairman of the Milken Institute Center for the Future of Aging, argues that, because the older are getting healthier and more active, society should rethink the notion of a retirement age.[61] The book humorously points out that if droves of 70-year-olds can dance like crazed teenagers in the front rows of a Rolling Stones concert, then they should be able to keep working as well. The idea would likely have seemed absurd to Einstein, who died in 1955 (aged 76), but it may not be so to Elan Musk, Bill Gates, or his aging friend, Warren Buffett.

The implications of an older and wiser workforce are mostly positive, if not transformative. To quote Mr. Irving, "if we learn to harness the benefits of longevity, the upside of aging will be realized and the world will be much better for it." Furthermore, as the number of healthier and more vibrant seniors multiplies, so too will the demand for a wider variety of fitness products, tourism, and leisure offerings. Such products and services will not only become more abundant, but also more sophisticated. The industrialist Marvin Davis was credited with saying, "as men get older, the toys get more expensive."

Beyond leisure and lifestyle, the healthcare industry is an obvious beneficiary of the trend towards aging. The World Health Organization's latest classification of diseases has grown to distinguish more than fifty thousand unique codes for diseases and injuries, with chronic diseases estimated to affect one out of every two adults, most of whom are older.[62] Prescription drug sales have been growing for decades, but the exploding availability of advanced cures and treatments should accelerate this growth, to the benefit of the aging consumers, as well as the pharmaceutical companies and care providers. Hospital utilization will also increase, as will the volume of patients receiving intensive care and undergoing complex surgeries and treatments, driving secular demand growth, particularly for medical consumables.

In summary, while the rapid aging of the population has some negative implications, we see many under-appreciated investment opportunities. Moreover, as believers in mankind's ability to innovate and adapt, we perceive the challenges ahead only as hurdles to be overcome, and not as reasons to be fearful.

24 DIGITIZATION

"Computers are useless. They can only give you answers."

Pablo Picasso

While we wouldn't exactly consider ourselves technophiles, we do agree with the authors of *The Second Machine Age*, who boldly claim that "we're at an inflection point – a point where the curve starts to bend a lot – because of computers."[63] If a new era is indeed upon us, then the chances of it being systematically under-appreciated by investors are reasonably high. "New era" themes are nothing new on Wall Street, so our excitement is somewhat guarded when it comes to predicting inflection points. That said, it is becoming harder to deny that secular growth in digital technologies, such as artificial intelligence, robotics, and data analytics, is accelerating – with profound implications for productivity and the future stock price performance of outstanding companies.

What intrigues us as investors is the notion that computers have already changed the world, yet their impact on aggregate productivity has been subtle or uneven at best, especially outside of the technology industry.

Not everyone is a believer that technology will drive productivity. One notable skeptic is Professor Robert J. Gordon of Northwestern University, who famously preached *The Death of Innovation* in a TED video posted in 2013, just as *The Second Machine Age* was being written. He is a pessimist who claims that the world's pace of technological innovation will not offset economic and demographic headwinds. The talk ends on a humorous note, with a slide of a toilet next to an iPhone, and a question for the audience: "If forced to choose, which one would you go for?"

While Professor Gordon's economic concerns are valid, we do not worry about the future contributions from technology. From what we can see, innovation has not slowed at all, but is in fact accelerating. We can accept that its influence on productivity has been restrained, but we think it has only been delayed and not altogether lost. In light of the tech bubble, the housing bubble, and the economic downturn of 2008 – all occurring within the last 20 years – productivity has naturally been under pressure. During the 1930s, even as the jet engine, nylon, and DDT were invented, US productivity actually declined. So, it is certainly not unprecedented for the benefits of innovation to be held back temporarily by economic turbulence.

Economic volatility is not the only explanation for the delayed benefit of technology. There are numerous documented cases of disruptive innovation actually hurting an industry's economics. The concept of *creative destruction*, first coined by the Austrian economist Joseph Schumpeter in the 1940s, provides a basic framework for explaining these headwinds.

In spite of its positive impacts, the view of innovation as the enemy has some merit. Many companies that embrace technology end up with higher costs and lower productivity than when they got started. What often separate winners from losers are cultural differences instead of the technologies themselves. If technological improvements are implemented by strong leaders and cooperative teams, then the odds of success are higher. The better a company can harness technology, the further it will pull away from the pack – whether in trucking, retailing, pest control, or any other industry.

The premise of *company plus machine* as a structural advantage is behind some of our best investment ideas. It is also the central point of another TED presentation, by Erik Brynjolfsson, co-author of *The Second Machine Age*, in which he claims that the key to growth is to team up humans with computers, and thereby *"race with the machines."* When Gary Gasparov lost the chess tournament to IBM's Deep Blue computer in 1997, it was thought that computers would subsequently dominate the world of competitive chess. The creation of "freestyle" chess tournaments shortly thereafter proved otherwise, as teams consisting of humans-plus-machines actually dominated the self-directed computers. Since IBM's Watson computer unseated the former champions of *Jeopardy!* in 2011, the same software has been deployed commercially in other endeavors, including the treatment of lung cancer at Memorial Sloan-Kettering Cancer Center. Watson is unlikely to replace humans, but it has already proven to enhance performance by transforming how people make critical decisions. The same dynamic applies to companies. Those that can truly harness the structural performance advantages of combining advanced machines with insightful humans will leap ahead of the rest. But, as the quote by Pablo Picasso suggests, unless the right human can ask the right questions at the right time, the computer will fail.

Digital growth is unique in that it is practically costless to produce, boundless in its spread, and exponential in its trajectory. Unlike the steam engine, which was physically constrained in its productive capacity, and more susceptible to the law of averages, progress under the new digital order is more likely to follow a *power-law* distribution. This concept is fully explored in a controversial 2013 book by economist Tyler Cowen titled *Average is Over*, which argues that because of technology, modern economies will polarize into a small minority who can exploit automated systems, and a vast majority that earn little and survive on low-priced goods created by the first group.[64]

While a "winner-take-all" outcome may carry negative social implications, we are optimistic about its investment implications. At the company level, we believe that the secular trend towards *digitization*, when combined with the advent of the *human-plus-machine* model, is a major driver of competitive advantage. The skeptics may ultimately prove right in terms of the averages; but that should not stop the outstanding companies from becoming even better by harnessing digital technology.

25 NETWORK EFFECTS

"Some things have to be believed to be seen."
Ralph Hodgson

Wikipedia defines *network effect* as "the effect that one user of a good or service has on the value of that product to other people." With the rapid growth of the internet since the early 1990s, and the leap in mobile connectivity more recently, the world is unquestionably a much larger network today than it was just a few years back. It is impossible to predict precisely what this will mean, but we can still recognize that tremendous value is likely to be unleashed as networks continue to expand.

In *The Rise and Fall of American Growth: The US*

Standard of Living since the Civil War, Robert Gordon profiles the impressive impact that great inventions like the automobile and the air conditioner had on US productivity and quality of life, before concluding that the internet has not, and will not, match those prior leaps in our standard of living.[65] *The Economist* gave the book a mixed review in the January 9, 2016 print edition, where they stated that Gordon "goes too far in downplaying the current I.T. revolution." Indeed, the terms *network effect,* *crowd sourcing,* and *mobile connectivity* don't even show up in the 762-page book, and neither does the recognition that the most valuable companies in the world are already network businesses.

One of the early hints that network effects were special was offered in 1980 by Robert Metcalfe, the inventor of the Ethernet, who observed in a technical presentation that the value of a telephone network grows nonlinearly as the number of subscribers to the network increases. The concept was popularized in the 1990s by George Gilder, publisher of a prominent dot-com-era newsletter that used to cite Metcalfe's Law when justifying the practice of attributing market value to cable miles and eyeballs.

While it may have been overused in the tech bubble, Metcalfe's Law has indeed survived the test of time as a valid rule of thumb for the evolving digital economy, with important implications to investors, corporate leaders, and policy makers. The internet is enabling a vast collection of rapidly-growing social and e-commerce networks for which the best investments might not be an obvious pick, but with a scale and scope that is certainly unprecedented. What Metcalfe's Law implies is that, contrary to Robert Gordon's assessment, tremendous value is being created by the growth of the internet, even if it has yet to be captured by the aggregate economic numbers.

The book *Platform Revolution*, which was published in March 2016, postulates that networks are indeed transforming the economy.[66] It explains how traditional, and presumably outdated, business models are reminiscent of pipelines, with a single line connecting input and output, while network businesses can have unlimited nodes and connections sprawling in all directions. The authors contend that the rules of strategy developed for pipeline businesses will no longer work in the network economy. Markets lacking niche specialization are particularly susceptible to disruption, while those that are regulated, or have high failure costs, are less vulnerable.

In a 2014 tweet, Aaron Levie, the 30-year old founder of Box, a cloud computing company that was started in 2005, wrote: "Sizing the market for a disruptor based on an incumbents market is like sizing the car industry off of how many horses there were in 1910." Indeed, because our minds are anchored to what we know, history is filled with examples of radical misjudgments regarding the future size of new markets. In a brilliant 2014 article titled *How to Miss by a Mile: An Alternative Look at Uber's Market Size*, venture capitalist Bill Gurley provides an example from 36 years ago to warn against predictions that are anchored in the past. "In 1980, McKinsey & Company was commissioned by AT&T (whose Bell Labs had invented telephony) to forecast cell phone penetration in the U.S. by 2000. The consultant's prediction, 900,000 subscribers, was less than 1% of the actual figure, 109 million. Based on this legendary mistake, AT&T decided there was not much future to these toys. A decade later, to rejoin the cellular market, AT&T had to acquire McCaw Cellular for $12.6 billion. By 2011, the number of subscribers worldwide had surpassed 5 billion and cellular communication had become an unprecedented technology revolution."

To be sure, the explosive growth in the value of networks has not been easy to fathom or detect. Alibaba, for instance, which didn't exist until 1999, these days handles over 80% of the e-commerce transactions in China, and was valued at over $230 billion upon coming public in September of 2014. It was the largest IPO in history, but some optimists are speculating that Uber, which started in 2009 and was valued at $62.5 billion in a subsequent capital raise, will smash that record when it eventually comes public. What both companies have in common is that they are pure networks disrupting traditional industries, and as Metcalfe's Law would have predicted, their value is expanding exponentially as they grow.

In closing, Metcalfe's Law implies that the impact from the recent explosion in connectivity will not be small. However, because we cannot predict future innovations, their future contributions to aggregate productivity and quality of life are also unknown. What we do know is that the internet continues to change our daily lives, as well as the way companies compete. We also know that the laws of supply and demand, and the cornerstones of value, will continue to apply. This is why we favor more established businesses with outstanding management, secular growth opportunities, and improving returns on capital, over startup concepts with aggressive growth targets. This is also the arena where even a more modest, yet still significant, benefit of Metcalfe's Law is likely to go unnoticed.

26 TECHNOLOGY

"When it is dark enough, you can see the stars."

Ralph Waldo Emerson

As behavioral economists have demonstrated time and again, our mind can be easily fooled by our own senses and emotions. Machines, on the other hand, can be much more efficient, and vastly superior to humans at processing information and taking swift actions. In light of our sensory and cognitive limitations, and aided by the growing confidence that we have in technology, there is no question that humans are becoming increasingly more reliant on digital data processing for making critical decisions. While there are obvious near-term benefits from this trend, the longer-term implications are not as clear. That algorithms cannot really think is not so much the problem, as is what happens when critical thinking becomes impossible without algorithms. Sometimes, as the Ralph Waldo Emerson quote suggests, too much data can hide the bigger picture.

For thousands of years, humans have synthesized a reasonable sense of reality based on a relatively limited data feed. Our biology is such that our sensory organs are quite limited, and very selective, in the data that they feed to our brains. Indeed, the electromagnetic spectrum alone is 10 million times larger than the portion that is visible to us. Bees, for instance, have much more powerful eyes than humans. Their compound eyes allow them to see colored electromagnetic fields well into the ultraviolet spectrum, which humans can't. However, if we were given a bee's eyes, or a dog's nose, or a bat's ears, it might just make it harder to focus.

In *Homo Deus: A brief History of Tomorrow*, historian Yuval Noah Harari claims that technology may be impairing our ability to rely on our own senses.[67] He gives the example of our sense of smell, which has lost much of its usefulness since the Stone Age. Whereas a hunter-gather's life depended on smell, the humans of today are more often bothered, than saved, by their noses. "Modern humanity," Harari observes, "is sick with FOMO – Fear Of Missing Out – and though we have more choices than ever before, we have lost the ability to really pay attention to whatever we choose." The implication is that while we may be able to upgrade our brain by use of ever more sophisticated sensors and data processing algorithms, this sort of progress may ultimately represent a downgrade of the human race. "As any farmer knows," he writes, "it's usually the brightest goat in the herd that stirs up the most trouble, which is why the Agricultural Revolution involved downgrading animal's mental abilities. The second cognitive revolution, dreamed up by techno-humanists, might do the same to us, producing human cogs who communicate and process data far more effectively than ever before, but who can barely pay attention, dream, or doubt." Harari's thesis is that humankind will ultimately morph into a single data processing system, which he calls the Internet-of-All-Things. "Once this mission is accomplished," he concludes, "*Homo Sapiens* will vanish."

While Harari's techno-theories might ring as extreme, his book offers important insights about the tendency for technology to take over our lives. He provides the example of Waze, the GPS-based navigation app, to illustrate how a powerful algorithm can go from being an all-knowing *oracle* to becoming a self-controlling *sovereign*. The Waze algorithm uses real-time traffic updates from millions of connected users in order to bring you to your destination through the quickest possible route. The better the technology works, the more users learn to trust it. With time and experience, this trust evolves to the point where users begin to depend on it blindly. However, as Harari warns, "when everybody uses the same oracle, and everybody believes the oracle, the oracle turns into a sovereign." If there is a traffic jam in one route, for instance, Waze cannot simply tell all the trusting users to take the alternative route, because then that route too will become jammed. Waze must think for itself, and perhaps instruct only some drivers to take the alternative route while keeping the information secret from the rest. As algorithms become increasingly tasked with deciding who gets what information and when, Harari fears that "the individual will transpire to be nothing but a religious fantasy."

Harari is not alone in worrying about technology. In his book, *Thank You for Being Late: An Optimistic Guide to Thriving in the Age of Accelerations,* journalist Thomas Friedman warns that we have no alternative but to embrace the exponential pace of change that technology engenders.[68] Friedman applies the popular analogies of bike riding and kayaking to the problem. The slower you go, the more vulnerable you are to losing your stability. "The only way to steer," he claims, "is to paddle as fast or faster than the rate of change in technology, globalization, and the environment." Indeed, a December 2015 study by McKinsey Global

Institute, titled *Digital America: A tale of the haves and have-mores*, found that the companies and individuals with the most sophisticated digital skills are expanding their lead over the rest of the economy at an accelerating pace.[69]   Friedman argues that this same phenomenon is playing out on a global basis.   "When Moore's law and globalization accelerate at their current rates and your country falls behind on education and infrastructure," he claims, "it falls behind at an accelerating rate as well."

In summary, while the hastened pace of technological change has both positive and negative implications, denying the trend does not appear to be a viable option. That said, the ability of technology to augment our senses and to help us with critical decisions might involve tradeoffs that are not always worth taking. In order to weigh these tradeoffs against their potential benefits, the onus is on us to think critically, and to focus on staying in control. As Warren Buffett has said about markets, technology too "must remain our servant, not our guide."

PART III

COGNITIVE BIASES

27 ANCHORING

"No man is happy but by comparison."

Thomas Shadwell

Wikipedia defines anchoring as a "cognitive bias that describes the common human tendency to rely too heavily on the first piece of information offered (the 'anchor') when making decisions." The concept was introduced in 1974 by Amos Tversky and Daniel Kahneman in a paper titled *Judgment Under Uncertainty: Heuristics and Biases.*[70] While they portrayed anchoring as a common and useful heuristic for making sense of the world, they also framed it as an inescapable and hazardous bias that corrupts our judgments.

How reliably people tend to fall for anchors has not

gone unnoticed in the field of marketing. For instance, it is a well-known trick for restaurant owners to add a remarkably expensive dish to the menu in order to drive up the overall check. *The Economist* uses a similar trick when it prices its *print + digital* offer next to the *print only* and the *digital only* options, all for the same price. Any rational being will not only prefer the *print + digital* alternative, but they will also tend to be irrationally attracted to the bargain.

In the book *Absolute Value*, Professor Itamar Simonson tells the story of how Williams Sonoma turned around sales of a particularly poor-selling bread maker by introducing a more expensive, less attractive version of the same product.[71] Simonson goes on to argue that the ability to manipulate consumers with such anchors has been diminished by the internet. In an online setting, he claims, an abundance of information will tend to weaken the impact of any one anchor in driving decisions. Indeed, while today's well-informed consumers are better guarded against the anchoring techniques that tripped up their less-informed predecessors, there is no doubting the influence of anchors on the online shopper.

Susceptibility to anchoring extends beyond the price-setting domain. As Psychology Professor Dan Ariely explains in the 2012 book titled *Predictably Irrational*, "we are always looking at the things around us in relation to others. We can't help it. This holds true not only for physical things – toasters, bicycles, puppies, restaurant entrees, and spouses – but for experiences such as vacations and educational options, and for ephemeral things as well: emotions, attitudes, and points of view. … We not only tend to compare things with one another but also tend to focus on comparing things that are easily comparable – and avoid comparing things that cannot be compared easily."[72] Ariely argues that some decisions that are inspired by easy anchors are often not even worth making. An attraction to GM, for instance, can be simply driven by the existence of Ford. Meanwhile, other perfectly good stocks might go neglected just because they lack an appropriate peer.

Corporations are just as susceptible to anchors as the individuals that run them. Ariely offers the case of exorbitant CEO pay as evidence of how anchoring wreaks havoc in the corporate world. "Once salaries became public information," he writes, referring to the SEC's new disclosure rules that went into effect in 1993, "the media regularly ran special stories ranking CEOs by pay. Rather than suppressing executive perks, the publicity has CEOs in America comparing their pay with that of everyone else." Much like consumers at a mall or patrons at a restaurant, companies will tend to spend more on executive compensation when higher-priced comparisons are made available. As

Ariely humorously comments, if everybody knew everybody else's pay, all but the highest-paid individuals would feel underpaid – and most would be looking for another job. As far as salaries go, perhaps it was Mark Twain who put it best when he said that "comparison is the death of joy."

Beyond prices and values, we are also biased by historical anchors. We go back in time to compare presidents and business cycles, wars and political regimes - and we invariably use these comparisons to draw distorted conclusions. In his seminal book about risk, *Against the Gods*, Peter Bernstein provides an example of this behavior in action.[73] "In the late 1950s," he writes, "a relationship sanctified by over eighty years of experience suddenly came apart when investors discovered that a thousand dollars invested in low-risk, high-grade bonds would, for the first time in history, produce more income than a thousand dollars invested in risky common stocks. In the early 1970s, long-term interest rates rose above 5% for the first time since the Civil War and have dared to *remain* above 5% ever since." Ironically, Bernstein's book was published in 1996, when it was practicably inconceivable that rates would proceed to fall for the next 20 years.

The anchoring effect may be difficult to dodge, but that doesn't keep people from trying. In an article posted on the subject in Psyblog, Dr. Jeremy Dean offers suggestions on how to avoid the negative influence of anchors.[74] His approach involves not only the gathering of as much information as possible before making decisions, but also trying to free oneself from the "anchor state" by thinking about other less-obvious comparisons. Whether it's with emotional matters or different forms of decision-making, thinking of alternative anchors under different contexts can indeed be helpful in identifying when our perception is being distorted by an anchor. As Dr. Dean explains, people tend to anchor to how they feel at the particular moment. This is what makes them feel like they will never be hungry again after having a good meal, or that they will never invest again after taking a big loss. Similarly, when faced with waves of bad news, people tend to think that it will never be good again. But as Warren Buffett reminds us, the time to be greedy is when others are fearful.

In summary, while anchoring provides a useful way for making sense of the world, it can also produce a distorted view of reality. As investors, we cannot avoid being tripped up by anchors, even when we acknowledge their existence. Yet, as the 17th century British playwright Thomas Shadwell must have also known, making no investment is unacceptable, at least by comparison.

28 HALO EFFECT

"The difference between a lady and a flower girl is not the way she behaves, but how she's treated."

George Bernard Shaw

The halo effect is a type of *confirmation bias*, wherein people tend to overlook contradicting evidence once their mind is made up. Wikipedia defines it as "a cognitive bias in which an observer's overall impression of a person, company, brand, or product influences the observer's feelings and thoughts about the entity's character or properties." Professor Edward Thorndike of Teachers College, Columbia University, coined the term in a 1920 paper titled *A Constant Error in Psychological Ratings.*[75] While Thorndike's work related to biases in the assessment of student aptitude, the term today applies more broadly to include products, companies, and concepts.

In *Blink*, Malcolm Gladwell warns of the halo effect as a caveat to the powers of rapid cognition.[76] He claims that people have a level of "unconscious prejudice" that they are not aware of, and that this bias affects the kinds of conclusions they reach about others. Gladwell pointed to the fact that most Fortune 500 CEOs are tall men as evidence that such a prejudice exists.

Work by Timothy Judge at the University of Florida supports Gladwell's observations. In a 2004 paper titled *The Effect of Physical Height on Workplace Success and Income*, he shows how "taller individuals are judged as being more persuasive, more attractive as mates, and more likely to emerge as a leader of other people." [77] Judge's observations about the halo effect of height extend beyond the workplace. He mentions how the last time the U.S. elected a president whose height was below average was in 1896. His point is not that voters tend to prefer tall men, but that such preferences are somehow wired into our subconscious.

The halo effect is not always a bad thing. As a heuristic, or rule of thumb, it can help people make objective decisions when confronted with incomplete or ambiguous information. A solid track record, for instance, can be a useful guide for new investors, much like a reputation for quality or strong customer service can drive sales of new products. The difficulty with halos, however, is that they can unknowingly distort the way we assess talent or reputation. A 1974 paper by Barry Staw of the University of Illinois demonstrated how this can happen.[78] In a controlled experiment, Staw asked groups of participants to estimate a company's future sales and earnings per share based on a set of financial data. Afterward, he told some groups they had performed well, and others that they had done poorly, regardless of the actual results. He then asked the participants to evaluate their groups on a variety of qualitative factors. When told they had performed well, people tended to describe their groups as having been highly capable, effective, and motivated. When told they had performed poorly, people tended to describe their groups as dysfunctional and unmotivated.

The halo effect can show up in many places, and it is particularly prominent in the business world. In a book titled *The Halo Effect*, Professor Phil Rosenzweig of Switzerland's International Institute for Management Development provides a wealth of examples of how the halo effect impacts our ability to determine what truly drives corporate excellence.[79] According to him, "so many of the things that we – managers, journalists, professors, and consultants – commonly think *contribute* to company performance are often attributions *based on* performance." To those attempting to understand what makes some companies thrive while others struggle, the halo effect is an essential consideration. But as Rosenzweig points out, most of the management books and academic research on this topic do not pay enough heed to the distortions caused by halos.

Rosenzweig tells the story of network gear provider Cisco Systems and Swiss-Swedish conglomerate ABB to illustrate how the halo effect can distort perceptions both positively and negatively over time. Prior to the bursting of the Nasdaq bubble, Cisco was highly admired for its culture, focus, and execution. After the technology cycle turned and the stock collapsed, however, the company was repeatedly criticized for lacking culture, straying from its core, and being the victim of poor execution. A similar fate struck ABB and its CEO, Percy Barnevik, who was widely revered in the 1990s while his company was performing well, only to be ostracized for his bloated pay package, misguided acquisitions, and bad leadership after the cycle turned against the company in the 2000s. Rosenzweig's point is that Cisco and ABB changed far less than the halo-induced swings in perception would imply.

In summary, the halo effect can distort our interpretation of reality by making things seem better, or worse, than they really are. In prospecting for outstanding companies, it is essential that we account for this effect by observing behaviors and perceptions during both good and bad times. Our goal as investors is not necessarily to avoid halos, but to determine when they are unjustified. To borrow from George Bernard Shaw, few opportunities are more rewarding than finding a *lady* when she is being treated as a *flower girl*.

29 VALUE TRAPS

"The color of truth is grey."

André Gide

The Financial Times defines a value trap as "a financial instrument that appears cheap on historical measures or valuation grounds, such as price to earnings ratio, but the price never recovers to fair value." What makes a value trap so difficult, even for the most patient investors, is that it can remain indistinguishable from a mistake for a very long time. As Warren Buffet has said, "price is what you pay, value is what you get".

The concept of a value trap goes beyond investing. In *Zen and the Art of Motorcycle Maintenance*, Robert Pirsig uses the behavior of South Indian monkeys to explain its nature.[80] When these monkeys stretch their arms deep into narrow holes to grab handfuls of rice left by the local villagers, their clutched fists no longer fit through the top of the hole, leaving them stuck to the ground. Of course, they could just release the food and go free, but monkeys place a high value on food. In fact, they place such a high value on it that they cannot force themselves to let go. Most will grip the rice tight until they die. While the story makes monkeys seem irrational, we all have our own equivalents to the rice. Clearly, not all rigidly held values are bad, but what works in one set of circumstances might not in others, and often the best course of action is to simply let go.

In *The Art of Execution*, money manager Lee Freeman-Shor classifies investors into three types based on how they deal with value traps.[81] The first type is the *rabbit*, who does nothing and ends up trapped in a hole. According to Freeman-Shor, rabbits are the least likely to recover from the trap. The second type is the *assassin*, who focuses on killing out losses before they turn into a trap. Such investors tend to lose less capital in a crisis, but they also lag in bull markets, and often miss out on their convictions. The third type is the *hunter*, who seeks to exit the trap by doubling down at more attractive prices. Freeman-Shor claims that both hunters and assassins can be solid investors over time, but that the rabbits often struggle to survive. The key message of the book is that, when it comes to value traps, you should not defer action for too long.

While there is no formula for coping with the contradictions and uncertainties that underpin any value trap, some interesting techniques have been proposed. In a Harvard Business Review article titled *How Successful Leaders Think*, Professor Roger Martin discusses the merits of what he calls *integrative thinking*.[82] According to Martin, "we were born with opposable minds, which allow us to hold two conflicting ideas in constructive, almost dialectic tension. We can use that tension to think our way toward new, superior ideas. Were we able to hold only one thought or idea in our heads at a time, we wouldn't have access to the insights that the opposable mind can produce." This framework applies neatly to the management of value traps, and Martin provides several business examples of the concept at play. His main point is that, by thinking differently, people can overcome biases to find solutions that would otherwise be unthinkable.

One reason why value traps are so difficult to exit from is that the human brain is wired to avoid actions that create regret. This phenomenon, known as the *disposition effect*, is what causes investors to hold their losers for longer than they should. They fear the possibility that they will regret having exited near the bottom. Research has confirmed that the disposition effect is particularly evident in the housing market, where the closely related *endowment effect* (or status quo bias) also runs strong. In a notable study of the Boston housing market in the 1990s, researchers demonstrated how home sellers facing a loss tend to list their property at substantial premiums to prevailing market prices, leading to a longer time on the market before they accept an offer.[83] The conclusion of the research seems obvious, but perhaps not to people trapped in their own homes.

In summary, with endeavors as complex as investing, it pays to stay flexible and open-minded with regards to value traps. While science can provide answers, it can also become the decoy that keeps us from noticing a trap for what it is. As the quote above implies, the truth is rarely obvious or one-sided.

30   NARROW FRAMING

"We suffer more in imagination than in reality."

Seneca

The term "narrow framing" was coined by Nobel Laureate Daniel Kahneman to describe the tendency for humans to treat choices one at a time, thereby resulting in flawed judgements. While the notion of framing biases has been around since the ancient days, its application to economic theory is relatively new, and its importance to investing is growing as information availability and human connectivity increase.

In a 1993 paper titled *Timid Choices and Bold Forecasts: A Cognitive Perspective on Risk Taking*, Kahneman and Lovallo argued that, while people are generally risk averse, they tend to be more risk-seeking in the domain of losses than in the domain of gains.[84] For instance, when offered a choice between a 50% chance to win $10,000 and a sure gain of $3,000, most people pick the sure thing; yet, when the choice is between a 50% chance of losing $10,000 and a sure loss of $3,000, most will take the gamble. The implication is that framing biases lead to decisions that are hard to justify on the basis of rationality.

An article in *Psychology Today* titled *Framing: Your Most Important and Least Recognized Daily Ment* highlighted the importance of framing to our everyday lives.[85] "There's a battle going on in your life," argues psychologist Noam Shpancer, "and it has major consequences for you – your health, your wealth, your feelings and behaviors – and yet you aren't even aware of it, even though it's happening mostly right inside your own brain. It's one of the fundamental struggles that define human existence: the framing battle." As behavioral finance research has confirmed, our minds react to the context in which something is embedded, not just the thing itself. This is why we don't "kill" sick dogs, but "put them to sleep;" why army commanders might instruct their troops to "improve their positions backwards" instead of "retreating;" and why portfolio managers often speak of "volatility" instead of "losses." Likewise, investors tend to prefer a 10% return on their investment in a country where inflation is 12% than settle for a 5% return where inflation is near zero.

In his 2015 book, *Misbehaving*, Richard Thaler describes how corporate managers systematically forego good opportunities because of narrow framing.[86] "Each manager is loss averse," he writes, "regarding any outcomes that will be attributed to him. In an organizational setting, the natural feeling of loss aversion can be exacerbated by the systems of rewards and punishment. In many companies, creating a large gain will lead to modest rewards, while creating an equal-sized loss will get you fired." As a result of being considered individually instead of as part of a broader strategy, fewer projects are undertaken than should be. One solution that Thaler proposes to this narrow framing problem is for companies to aggregate investments into a pool in which they can be evaluated as a portfolio, with managers being rewarded for the aggregate success of the package rather than the outcome of any single, risky project.

Just as it can lead companies to underperform, narrow framing can compel investors to overtrade and underinvest. In a 1997 experiment by Thaler, Kahneman, and Tversky, student subjects at Berkeley were asked to invest the capital of a university endowment. Some subjects were given access to their results eight times per simulated calendar year, while others were only permitted to visit their results once a year or once every five years. As predicted by theory, those who saw their results with greater frequency tended to be more cautious and less able to escape the debilitating effects of narrow framing.

In the 2010 book *What Technology Wants*, Kevin Kelly provides an example of how a broader view can be helpful in framing a subject as complex as the future of technology.[87] "On the much smaller day-to-day scale," he writes, "predicting the future of technology is impossible. It's too hard to filter out the random noise of commerce. We will have better luck extrapolating historical trends that in some cases go back billions of years to see how they arc through technology today. These trends are subtle, nudging technologies in a slow drift in one direction that may not even be visible in the blink of a year."

Kelly borrows from theologian James Carse in framing life in terms of finite and infinite games. "Finite games," he explains, "are dramatic; think sports and war." Infinite games, on the other hand, continue endlessly with less drama. Peace, he claims, is an infinite game. "Peace is summoned all over the world because it births increasing opportunity and, unlike a finite game, contains infinite potential." The goal in an infinite game is to keep playing. Kelly believes technology is an infinite game that will "populate the world with all conceivable ways of comprehending the infinite." "Conflict, disaster, things unraveling," Kelly observed in a July 2016 interview with Smithsonian.com, "are much more cinematic and make a better story than things working smoothly, which is basically boring. … We can imagine how things might go wrong, but it's much more likely that things will go well."

In summary, frames exert a greater impact on us than we tend to realize. The way we frame a problem can affect our ability to find a solution, just as the way we frame a portfolio can affect our willingness to bear necessary risk. While its hazards are well known, the act of framing cannot be avoided. As such, when searching for long-term compounding, the onus is on us to ensure that our frames are neither too few nor too narrow.

31 MORAL HAZARD

"Trust, but verify."

Ronald Reagan

When it was first used in the fire insurance industry during the 19th century, the term *moral hazard* referred to the risk of insuring bad characters. People who were labeled as dishonest were typically denied insurance, and contracts that were thought to create a temptation to cheat were generally not written. Nowadays, the term refers less to moral considerations and focuses more on economic incentives and conflicts.

Moral hazard took on this modern meaning during the 1970s, after economists Kenneth Arrow and Joseph Stiglitz explained it in terms of the principal-agent problem.[88]   According to that framework, moral hazard results from information asymmetry and conflicts of interest between principals and their agents. The payment of a tip offers a good example of this theory in action. A waiter (the agent) is incentivized by the prospect of a good tip to provide great service to his customers (the principals). In the hope of maximizing his tip, however, the waiter might offer free drinks, thereby cutting into the restaurant's profits. In this particular case, the tip itself becomes a moral hazard to the waiter, who is motivated to act in his own best interest, even when it goes against the interest of his other principal, the restaurant owner.

From public policy to sports to business management, evidence of moral hazard is not hard to find. In a 2012 paper, the General Aviation Revitalization Act of 1994 was cited as the main reason for a reduction in the number of accidents involving old, privately owned aircraft. According to this research, the limitation of manufacturer's liability incentivized the owners of such aircraft to exercise greater caution than before the law was changed.[89]   Conversely, a 2014 *Washington Post* editorial explains how the US National Flood Insurance Program (NFIP), which sells subsidized coverage against inundation for homes and businesses, continues to be a major source of moral hazard, as it encourages irresponsible construction in flood zones.[90]   Another study, published in the

August 2003 issue of *The Review of Economics and Statistics*, analyzed the contracts of 1,873 NFL players between 1986 and 1995 and concluded that moral hazard caused professional players to play harder near the expirations of their contracts.[91] This same breed of moral hazard crops up on Wall Street as bonus season approaches and at publicly owned corporations ahead of options grants.

While it is sometimes hard to spot, moral hazard is endemic among publicly owned corporations. This is because the interest of shareholders (the principals) is not always aligned with those of the managers (the agents), and sometimes not even with those of the board of directors, whose responsibility is to police the agents. In light of the information asymmetry that exists, the misalignment of a CEO's self-interest with those of owners often results in moral hazard. Earnings manipulation, excessive pay, ill-conceived acquisitions, and under-investment are just a few examples of what can happen when moral hazard gets the upper hand.

While conflict of interest is a common source of moral hazard, it is not the only context in which the concept applies. In a book titled *Snow Sense: A Guide to Evaluating Snow Avalanche Hazard*, avalanche expert Jill Fredston explains how more sophisticated avalanche safety gear can become a moral hazard.[92] "If you let your gear make you feel safer," she writes, "you are more likely to act in less safe ways that increase your chances of getting into trouble." She also highlights the risk of hiking in big groups. "While we feel safer in herds, the reality is that big groups actually decrease our safety because it is difficult to communicate, make objective decisions, and follow safe travel procedures. The bigger the group, the more emboldened we are likely to be."

Fredston also warns against the hazards inherent in becoming complacent about the status quo: "Because the snowpack is stable most of the time, it is common to travel to a particular spot in avalanche terrain repeatedly without seeing any avalanches. As a result, we get 'positive reinforcement,' that is, we begin to think of an area as safe. But if we visit that location often enough, sooner or later we will encounter unstable conditions." Not surprisingly, her method for coping with this hazard requires a deep understanding of what causes an avalanche and incessant verification of the facts. As they say in pilot training, "safety is no accident."

In his 2008 letter to shareholders, Warren Buffett echoed Fredston's warning.[93] "Clinging to cash equivalents or long-term government bonds at present yields," he wrote, "is almost certainly a terrible policy if continued for long. Holders of these instruments, of course, have felt increasingly comfortable — in fact, almost smug — in following this policy as financial turmoil has mounted. They regard their judgment confirmed when they hear commentators proclaim 'cash is king,' even though that wonderful cash is earning close to nothing and will surely find its purchasing power eroded over time. Approval, though, is not the goal of investing. In fact, approval is often counter-productive because it sedates the brain and makes it less receptive to new facts or a re-examination of conclusions formed earlier. Beware the investment activity that produces applause; the great moves are usually greeted by yawns."

In summary, moral hazards run rampant throughout society and particularly in markets where information asymmetry and conflicts of interest exist. When we prospect for outstanding companies and managements, the question of moral hazard is an important consideration. Our approach to the problem is only slightly different from President Reagan's: we verify closely before we trust, and then we verify again and again.

32 GOODHART'S LAW

"What we observe is not nature itself, but nature exposed to our method of questioning."

Werner Heisenberg

According to Wikipedia, *Goodhart's law* states that when a measure becomes a target, it stops being a good measure. While measurements and targets are essential in managing complex systems, bad interpretations of reality and the flawed decisions they inspire can result from ignoring this simple law.

Charles Goodhart introduced his law in a 1975 paper titled *Problems of Monetary Management: The UK Experience*, in which he argued that a policy of monetary targeting by the Bank of England had been inappropriate and should therefore be abandoned.[94] "As soon as the government attempts to regulate any particular set of financial assets," Goodhart stated, "these become unreliable indicators of economic trend."

Some have argued that the law is essentially the social science equivalent of physicist Werner Heisenberg's *uncertainty principle,* which was introduced in the 1920s. In its simplest interpretation, Heisenberg's principle proposes that a system cannot be observed without also being disturbed. In fact, this observation applies as well to inflation targeting, election polls, standardized tests, and earnings management as it does to quantum particles.

Contemporary examples of Goodhart's law in action are plentiful. The September 24, 2016 issue of *The Economist*, for instance, ran an article titled *Why Bad Science Persists*, which blamed a flawed system of incentives for a persistent abundance of bogus scientific research. Quoting a recent paper by Paul Smaldino of the University of California and Richard McElreath at the Max Planck Institute, the article states that when a laboratory's success is determined by its ability to publish in large volumes, then the system will favor those that are able to cut corners. They proceed to conclude that "the way to end the proliferation of bad science is not to nag people to behave better, or even to encourage replication, but for universities and funding agencies to stop rewarding researchers who publish copiously over those who publish fewer, but perhaps higher-quality papers." In other words, the article advocates avoiding undue focus on any specific target, concentrating, instead, on the overall quality of the research. This is, essentially, what Goodhart's law would dictate.

In an extreme example of how targeting a given metric can make such metric dangerously misleading, a June 2010 piece in the *New York Times* titled *Under Pressure, Teachers Tamper with Tests* blames the targeting of test results as a measure of school performance for the increase in the incidence of institutionalized cheating by educators.[95] To quote the article: "Of all the forms of academic cheating, none may be as startling as educators tampering with children's standardized tests. However, investigations in Georgia, Indiana, Massachusetts, Nevada, Virginia and elsewhere this year have pointed to cheating by educators. Experts say the phenomenon is increasing as the stakes over standardized testing ratchet higher — including, most recently, taking student progress on tests into consideration in teachers' performance reviews." In this case, a seemingly well-intentioned policy designed to improve national education, ended up by producing the opposite result.

Perhaps the best-known tale of Goodhart's law in action is that of the Soviet nail factory which was blindly managed to meet quotas. When central planners set the factory's quotas by *quantity*, it churned out hundreds of thousands of tiny, useless nails. Upon being informed of the problem, the planners dutifully abandoned the volume-based quota in favor of a weight-based one, which resulted in the production of oversized individual nails that were equally useless. The bottom line is that the unilateral targeting of one metric or another often fails to produce the desired outcome. A similar phenomenon takes hold when portfolio managers target a particular portfolio metric without careful consideration of why and when it should or should not work.

The book *Capital Returns*, which compiles a collection of essays by the co-founders of global investment firm Marathon Asset Management, shows how investors can also be vulnerable to Goodhart's law.[96] They tell the story of Ahold, the infamous Dutch food retailer that would come to be known as Europe's Enron. Prior to the eruption of the accounting scandal in 2003, Ahold had been celebrated for achieving 23 consecutive quarters of double-digit EPS growth. Indeed, the management of Ahold was unwavering in its focus on EPS, as were the many analysts that followed it. The lesson that Marathon derives from the Ahold case is not that EPS is useless, but that once it becomes a closely followed target, it can itself distort value. Those who focus on any given metric too intensely are less likely to appreciate the very property that such metric was design to capture.

In summary, targets have a bigger impact on metrics than is often appreciated. While there is no lack of strategies for identifying relevant metrics that can be used as targets, less attention is paid to how such targets impact actual performance and vice versa. When a company places undue attention on any particular metric, the onus befalls to the investor to consider whether the metric has lost its relevance or, worse yet, has become an instigator of bad decisions. As Heisenberg must have surmised, everything is relative. What he may not have appreciated, though, is how well his insights on quantum physics would apply to investing.

33   NEGATIVITY BIAS

"The future influences the present just as much as the past."

Friedrich Nietzsche

Wikipedia defines negativity bias as "the notion that, even when of equal intensity, things of a more negative nature have a greater effect on one's psychological state and processes than do neutral or positive things."   While a measured dose of pessimism can be helpful in managing risk, the negativity bias, when left unchecked, is one of the biggest obstacles to long-term compounding.

In an often-cited academic paper titled *Bad is Stronger than Good*, the authors review a vast body of research in which psychological experiments were used to verify the hypothesis that humans are hard-wired to be negative.[97]   They claim that negative events cause people to engage in a greater search for meaning than positive events and that this search can, in turn, reinforce the negativity to irrational levels.

Throughout history, and across a broad range of financial and social conditions, humans have wrestled with a seemingly unique and profound fear of the future. No matter how good a particular past may seem in hindsight, it is always possible to find people who were just as frightened of the future then, as many are today. Consider the early years of the great bull market that ran from the 1980s through 2000. Who would have guessed in the mid-80s, when the US and the Soviet Union had enough nuclear weapons pointed at each other to wipe out the planet at the push of a button, that stocks would keep compounding at double-digit rates for the next twenty years? All the time and energy that was spent worrying about nuclear war may have helped to avoid it, but it didn't help you stay invested in stocks.

In *The Science of Fear*, reporter and author Daniel Gardner claims that modern humans inherited the fear instinct from their cave-dwelling ancestors.[98] "If the history of our species were written in proportion to the amount of time we lived at each stage of development," he writes, "two hundred pages would be devoted to the lives of nomadic hunter-gatherers. One page would cover agrarian societies. The world of the last two centuries – the modern world – would get one short paragraph at the end." The main point of his book is that, while the fear mechanism that evolved in humans may have been valuable in coping with risk in prehistoric times, it is not so useful with many of the new challenges presented by the modern world. Thanks to the internet, Gardner concludes, the culture of fear that results from our negativity bias may be getting stronger, even while our collective quality of life continues to improve.

Gardner's book provided a wealth of examples on how the media's negativity bias amplifies the public's fear, often to levels that are disconnected with reality. The media is naturally biased towards negative news, because that is what their readers want to read. As Gardner puts it: "More fear, more reporting. More reporting, more fear. Like a microphone held too close to the loudspeaker, modern media and the primal human brain create a feedback loop." It is not surprising, then, that the title of the most read article on Bloomberg in 2015 was a doom-filled one: *S&P Corrects, Oil Routed as Selloff in Risk Assets Deepens*. This particular article ran on August 24th, just one day before the S&P 500 registered its lowest close of the year.

A common form by which the media exaggerates

risk is what Gardner calls *denominator blindness*. He gives the example of an editorial in *The Times* of London claiming that the number of British people murdered by strangers had increased by a third in eight years. "Most people would find that at least a little scary. Certainly, the editorial writers did. But what the editorial did not say is that there are roughly 60 million Britons, and so the chance of being murdered by a stranger rose from 99 in 60 million to 130 in 60 million. Do the math and the risk is revealed to have risen from an almost invisible 0.0001 percent to an almost invisible 0.00015 percent."

The way that the market reacts to good news says a lot about investor sentiment. In a 2005 book titled *Anatomy of the Bear*, Russell Napier draws lessons from Wall Street's great bear markets with the ambitious, if not illusive, goal of spotting the next bottom.[99] By studying contemporary media reports, Napier exposes the myth that stock market lows lead economic recoveries by six to nine months. Instead, he shows how economic improvement and better news in the media actually led the four major, 20th-century bottoms of 1921, 1932, 1949, and 1982. Napier concludes that "bear market bottoms are characterized by an increasing supply of good economic news being ignored by the market."

As risk managers, we cannot ignore our fear of the

future.   After all, being scared is safer than being bold.   That said, serial compounding accrues only to those who have the courage to stay invested, in spite of their fears.   There is no single formula for dealing with fear, but an investment process should not revolve around it. If we spend most of our time researching what we fear, we are less likely to find the better opportunities.

In summary, to be negative is human, yet investing for the long-run demands a counter-dose of optimism.   Awareness, critical thinking, and a diligent process all count, but as Nietzsche would agree, a view of the future that is too negative is likely to produce a negative result in the present.

BIBLIOGRAPHY

[1] Silver, Nate. *The Signal and the Noise: Why most fail but some don't.* USA: The Penguin Press, 2012.

[2] Marks, Howard. *The Most Important Thing: Uncommon Sense for the Thoughtful Investor.* West Sussex, NY: Columbia University Press, 2011.

[3] Tetlock, Philip. *Expert Political Judgement: How Good is It? How Can We Know?* Princeton, NJ: Princeton University Press, 2005.

[4] Reamer, Norton and Jesse Downing. *Investment: A History.* New York: Columbia Business School Press, 2016.

[5] Kay, John. *Obliquity: Why Our Goals Are Best Achieved Indirectly.* New York: Penguin Books, 2012.

[6] Kaiser, Keven and S. David Young. *The Blue Line Imperative: What Managing for Value Really Means.* San Francisco: John Wiley & Sons, 2013.

[7] Zook, Chris and James Allen. *Repeatability: Build enduring businesses for a world of constant change.* USA: Bain and Company, Inc., 2012.

8 Miller, Peter. *The Genius of Swarms.* National Geographic Magazine. July 2007 issue.

9 Perkins, Dennis N. T. with Margaret P. Holtman and Jillian B. Murphy. *Leading at The Edge: Leadership Lessons from the Extraordinary Saga of Shackleton's Antarctic Expedition.* New York: American Management Association (AMACOM), 2012.

10 Ahmad, Christopher S. *SKILL: 40 Principles that Surgeons, Athletes, and other Elite Performers Use to Achieve Mastery.* USA: Lead Player LLC, 2015.

11 Csíkszentmihályi, Mihály. *Flow: The Psychology of Optimal Experience.* USA: Harper Perennial Modern Classics, 2008.

12 Chambliss, Daniel F., *The Mundanity of Excellence: An Ethnographic Report on Stratification and Olympic Swimmers.* Sociology Theory, Vol. 7, No. 1, 70-86. USA: Hamilton Digital Commons, 1989.

13 Tyler, Edward B. *Primitive Culture: Researches Into the Development of Mythology, Philosophy, Religion, Art, and Custom, Volume 1.* USA: J. Murray, 1871.

14 Schein, Edgar H. *The Corporate Culture Survival Guide.* USA: Jossey-Bass, 2009.

[15] Tett, Gillian. *The Silo Effect: The Peril of Expertise and the Promise of Breaking Down Barriers.* New York: Simon and Schuster, 2016.

[16] Duckworth, Angela. *Grit: The Power of Passion and Perseverance.* USA: Scribner, 2016.

[17] Boczkowski, Pablo J. *News at Work: Imitation in an Age of Information Abundance.* Chicago: University of Chicago Press, 2010.

[18] Koller, Tim Richard Dobbs, Bill Huyett and McKinsey & Company. *Value: The Four Cornerstones of Corporate Finance.* New Jersey: John Wiley & Sons, 2011.

[19] Mauboussin, Michael J. *More than You Know: Finding Financial Wisdom in Unconventional Places.* New York: Columbia Business School Press, 2013.

[20] Fearon, Scott and Jesse Powell. *Dead Company Walking: How a Hedge Fund Manager Finds Opportunity in Unexpected Places.* New York: St. Martin's Press, 2015.

[21] Bosk, Charles. *Forgive and Remember: Managing Medical Failure.* Chicago: University of Chicago Press, 2003.

[22] Kraik, Kenneth. *The Nature of Explanation.* England. Cambridge University Press, 1967.

[23] Damodaran, Aswath. *Narrative and Numbers: The Value of Stories in Business.* New York: Columbia University Press, 2017.

[24] Kilts, James. *Doing What Matters.* USA: Crown Business, 2010.

[25] Shiller, Robert. *Narrative Economics.* Cowles Foundation Discussion Paper No. 2069. Yale University, January 2017.

[26] Darwin, Charles. *The Origin of Species.* New York: P. F. Collier & Son, 1909.

[27] Siegel, Alan and Irene Etzkorn. *Simple: Conquering the Crisis of Complexity.* USA: Twelve, 2013.

[28] Iyengar, Sheena. *The Art of Choosing.* New York: Hachette Books Group, 2010.

[29] Portnoy, Brian. *The Investor's Paradox: The Power of Simplicity in a World of Overwhelming Choice.* USA: Palgrave Macmillan, 2014.

[30] Watts, Duncan. *Everything is Obvious: Once you Know the Answer.* USA: Crown Business, 2011.

[31] Roth, Benjamin. *The Great Depression: A Diary.* USA: Public Affairs, 2010.

[32] Fisher, Ken with Elisabeth Dellinger. *Beat the Crowd: How You Can Out-Invest the Herd by Thinking Differently.* New Jersey: Wiley, 2015.

[33] Burdick, Alan. *Why Time Flies: A Mostly Scientific Investigation.* New York: Simon & Schuster, 2017.

[34] Quoidbach, Gilbert, and Wilson. *The End of History Illusion.* Science, Vol. 339, Issue 6115, January 2013.

[35] Mischel, Walter. *The Marshmallow Test: Why Self-Control is the Engine of Success.* USA: Back Boys Books, 2015.

[36] Thiel, Peter. *Zero to One: Notes on Startups, or How to Build the Future.* New York: Penguin Random House, 2014.

[37] Waitzkin, Josh. *The Art of Learning: An Inner Journey to Optimal Performance.* New York: Simon and Schuster Inc., 2007.

[38] Emanuel, Ezekiel. Reinventing American Health Care: How the Affordable Care Act Will Improve our Terribly Complex, Blatantly Unjust, Outrageously Expensive, Grossly Inefficient, Error Prone System. New York, NY. Public Affairs, 2014.

[39] Mauboussin, Michael J. *The Success Equation: Untangling Skill and Luck in Business, Sports, and Investing*. Boston: Harvard Business Review Press, 2012.

[40] Gould, Stephen Jay. *Full House: The Spread of Excellence from Plato to Darwin*. New York: Random House, 1996.

[41] Grantham, Jeremy. *Grantham Calls the Next Market Top*. Barron's, November 18, 2014 issue.

[42] Dawkins, Richard. *The Selfish Gene*. England: Oxford University, 1978.

[43] Berger, Jonah. *Contagious: Why Things Catch On*. New York: Farrar, Straus and Giroux, 2016.

[44] Kahneman, Daniel. *Thinking, Fast and Slow*. New York: Farrar, Straus and Giroux, 2013.

[45] Taleb, Nassim Nicholas. *The Black Swan: The Impact of the Highly Improbable*. New York: Random House, 2010.

[46] Christensen, Clayton and Michael E. Raynor. *The Innovator's Solution: Creating and Sustaining Successful Growth*. Boston: Harvard Business review Press, 2013.

[47] Knight, Frank H. *Risk, Uncertainty, and Profit*. Florida: Signalman Publishing, 1921.

48 King, Mervyn. *The End of Alchemy: Money, Banking, and the Future of the Global Economy.* New York: W. W. Norton & Company, 2016.

49 Simon, Herbert A. *Administrative Behavior: A Study of Decision-Making Processes in Administrative Organization.* New York: Macmillan, 1947.

50 Friedman, Milton. *The Methodology of Positive Economics.* USA: University of Chicago Press, 1966.

51 Mandelbrot, Benoit and Richard L. Hudson. *The Misbehavior of Markets: A Fractal View of Financial Turbulence.* New York: Basic Books, 2004.

52 Hock, Dee. *Birth of the Chaordic Age.* San Francisco, CA: Berrett-Koehler Publishers, Inc., 1999.

53 Surowiecki, James. *The Wisdom of Crowds.* New York: Random House, 2005.

54 Ball, Philip. *Critical Mass: How One Thing Leads to Another.* New York: Farrar, Straus and Giroux, 2006.

55 Buffett, Warren. *Berkshire Hathaway Letters to Shareholders, 2012.*

[56] Taleb, Nassim Nicholas. *Antifragile: Things That Gain from Disorder.* New York: Random House, 2012.

[57] Siegel, Jeremy J. *Stocks for the Long Run: The Definitive Guide to Financial Market Returns & Long-Term Investment Strategies.* NY: McGraw-Hill Education, 1994.

[58] Siegel, Jeremy J. *The Future for Investors: Why the Tried and the True Triumph Over the Bold and the New.* New York. Random House, 2005.

[59] Schmidt, Eric and Jared Cohen. *The New Digital Age: Transforming Nations, Businesses, and our lives.* New York: Random House LLC., 2014.

[60] Easterbrook, Gregg. *What Happens When We All Live to 100?* The Atlantic. October 2014 issue.

[61] Irving, Paul H. *The Upside of Aging: How Long Life Is Changing the World of Health, Work, Innovation, Policy and Purpose.* Hoboken, NJ: John Wiley & Sons, Inc. 2014.

[62] World Health Organization. *International Classification of Diseases (ICD-11).* Geneva: June, 2018.

[63] Brynjolfsson, Erik and Andrew McAfee. *The Second Machine Age: Work, Progress, and Prosperity in a Time of Brilliant Technologies.* New York: W. W. Norton & Company, Inc., 2014.

[64] Cowen, Tyler. *Average is Over: Powering America Beyond the Age of Great Stagnation.* New York: Penguin Group, 2013.

[65] Gordon, Robert J. *The Rise and Fall of American Growth: The U.S. Standard of Living since the Civil War.* New Jersey: The Princeton University Press, 2016.

[66] Parker, Geoffrey G., Marshall W. Van Alstyne and Sangeet Paul Choudary. *Platform Revolution: How Networked Markets Are Transforming the Economy – And How to Make Them Work for You.* New York: W. W. Norton & Company, 2016.

[67] Harari, Yuval. *Homo Deus: A Brief History of Tomorrow.* New York: Harper, 2017.

[68] Friedman, Thomas. *Thank You for Being Late: An Optimist's Guide to Thriving in the Age of Accelerations.* New York: Farrar, Straus and Giroux, 2016.

[69] Manyika, James, Sree Ramaswamy, Somesh Khanna, Hugo Sarrazin, Gary Pinkus, Guru Sethupathy, and Andrew Yaffe. *Digital America: A Tale of the Haves and Have-Mores*. McKinsey Global Institute, December 2015.

[70] Tversky, Amos and Daniel Kahneman. *Judgment Under Uncertainty: Heuristics and Biases.* American Association for the Advancement of Science, Vol. 85, No. 4157, September 1994.

[71] Simonson, Itamar and Emanuel Rosen. *Absolute Value: What Really Influences Customers in the Age of (Nearly) Perfect Information*. New York: Harper Business, 2014.

[72] Ariely, Dan. *Predictably Irrational: The Hidden Forces that Shape Our Decisions*. USA: Harper Perennial, 2010.

[73] Bernstein, Peter L. *Against the Gods: The Remarkable Story of Risk*. USA: Wiley, 1998.

[74] Dean, Jeremy. *Anchoring Effect: How the Mind is Biased by First Impressions*. Psyblog website, August 2013.

[75] Thorndike, Edward. *A Constant Error in Psychological Ratings*. Journal of Applied Psychology, Vol. 4, No. 1, March 1920.

[76] Gladwell, Malcolm. *Blink: The Power of Thinking without Thinking.* USA: Back Bay Books, 2007.

[77] Judge, Timothy and Daniel Cable. *The Effect of Physical Height on Workplace Success and Income: Preliminary Test of a Theoretical Model.* Journal of Applied Psychology. 2004, Vol. 89, No. 3, 428-441.

[78] Staw, Barry M. *Attitudinal and Behavioral Consequences of Changing a Major Organizational Reward: A natural field experiment.* Journal of Personality & Social Psychology, 1974.

[79] Rosenzweig, Phil. *The Halo Effect: ...and the Eight Other Business Delusions that Deceive Managers.* USA: Free Press, 2014.

[80] Pirsig, Robert M. *Zen and the Art of Motorcycle Maintenance: An Inquiry into Values.* New York: Harper Collins, 2006.

[81] Freeman-Shor, Lee. *The Art of Execution: How the world's best investors get it wrong and still make millions.* USA: Harriman House, 2015.

[82] Martin, Roger L. *How Successful Leaders Think.* Harvard Business Review, June 2007 issue.

[83] Genesove, David and Christopher Mayer. *Loss Aversion and Seller Behavior: Evidence from the Housing Market.* Hebrew University of Jerusalem, March 2000.

[84] Kahneman, Daniel and Dan Lovallo. *Timid Choices and Bold Forecasts: A Cognitive Perspective on Risk Taking.* Management Science, Vol. 39, No. 1, January 1993.

[85] Shpancer, Noam. *Framing: Your Most Important and Least Recognized Daily Ment.* Psychology Today, December 2010.

[86] Thaler, Richard H. *Misbehaving: The Making of Behavioral Economics.* New York: W. W. Norton & Company, 2016.

[87] Kelly, Kevin. *What Technology Wants.* New York: Penguin Books, 2011.

[88] Baker, Tom. *On the Genealogy of Moral Hazard.* Texas Law Review, Vol. 75, No. 2, December 1996.

[89] Helland, Eric and Alexander Tabarrok. *Product Liability and Moral Hazard: Evidence from General Aviation.* Journal of Law and Economics, Vol. 55, No. 3, August 2012.

[90] *Hold strong on flood insurance.* Washington Post Editorial, February 2, 2014 issue.

[91] Conlin, Michael and Patrick M. Emerson. *Multidimensional Separating Equilibria and Moral Hazard: And Empirical Study of National Football League Contract Negotiations.* The Review of Economic Statistics, Vol. 85, No. 3, August 2003.

[92] Fredston, Jill and Doug Fesler. *Snow Sense: A Guide to Evaluating Snow Avalanche Hazard*. USA: Alaska Mountain Safety Center, 2011.

[93] Buffett, Warren. *Berkshire Hathaway Letters to Shareholders, 2008*.

[94] Goodhart, Charles. *Problems of Monetary Management: The U.K. Experience*. Papers in Monetary Economics, Reserve Bank of Australia, 1975.

[95] Gabriel, Trip. *Under Pressure, Teachers Tamper With Tests*. New York Times article. June 10, 2010.

[96] Chancellor, Edward. *Capital Returns: Investing Through the Capital Cycle: A Money Manager's Reports 2002-15*. USA: Palgrave Macmillan, 2015.

[97] Baumeister, Bratslavsky, Finkenauer, and Vohs. *Bad Is Stronger Than Good*. Review of General Psychology, 2001. Vol. 5. No. 4 323-370.

[98] Gardner, Daniel. *The Science of Fear: How the Culture of Fear Manipulates Your Brain*. USA: Plume Books, 2009.

[99] Napier, Russell. *Anatomy of the Bear: Lessons from Wall Street's Four Great Bottoms*. New York: Harriman House, 2007.

RECOMMENDED BOOKS (by Topic)

Investing

Benello, Allen, Michael van Biema, and Tobias Carlisle. *Concentrated Investing: Strategies of the World's Greatest Concentrated Value Investors*. New Jersey: John Wiley & Sons, 2016.

Biggs, Barton. *Diary of a Hedgehog: Biggs' Final Words on the Market*. New Jersey: John Wiley & Sons, 2012.

Biggs, Barton. *A Hedge Fund Tale of Reach and Grasp*. New Jersey: John Wiley & Sons, 2011.

Brilliant, Heather and Elizabeth Collins. *Why Moats Matter: The Morningstar Approach to Stock Investing*. New Jersey: John Wiley &Sons, 2014.

Christensen, Clayton M. *The Innovator's Dilemma: When New Technologies Cause Great Firms to Fail (Management of Innovation and Change)*. Boston: Harvard Business Review Press, 2016

Cunningham, Lawrence, Torkell T. Eide and Patrick Hargreaves. *Quality Investing: Owning the Best Companies for the Long Term*. USA: Harriman House; 1st edition, 2016.

Davis, Ned. *Being Right or Making Money.* New York: John Wiley & Sons, 2014.

Davis, Ned. *The Triumph of Contrarian Investing: Crowds, Manias, and Beating the Market by Going Against the Grain.* New York: McGraw-Hill, 2004.

Davis, Ned. *Beware of the Crowd at Extremes: The Importance of Contrary Thinking.* Privately printed by Ned Davis Research, 2003.

Dickson, Watts G. *Speculation as a Fine Art and Thoughts on Life.* USA: Fraser Publishing Company, 1965.

Dreman, David N. *Psychology and the Stock Market: Investment Strategies Beyond Random Walk.* New York: Amacom, 1977.

Easterling, Ed. *Unexpected Returns: Understanding Secular Stock Market Cycles.* USA: Cypress House, 2005.

Edwards, Robert D. and John Magee. *Technical Analysis of Stock Trends (8th Edition).* USA: St. Lucie Press, 2001.

Einhorn, David. *Fooling Some of the People All of the Time: A Long Short Story.* New York: John Wiley & Sons, 2008.

Faber, Marc. *Tomorrow's Gold: Asia's Age of Discovery.* Hong Kong: CSLA Books, 2002.

Fisher, Ken. *The Only Three Questions that Count: Investing by Knowing What Others Don't.* New York: John Wiley & Sons, 2012.

Fisher, Philip A. *Common Stocks and Uncommon Profits.* USA: Harper & Brothers, 1958.

Fishman, Ray and Tim Sullivan. *The Inner Lives of Markets: How People Shape Them – And They Shape Us.* USA: Perseus Books Group, 2016.

Graham, Benjamin. *The Intelligent Investor [1949].* New York: Harper Business, 2013.

Graham, Benjamin and David L. Dodd. *Security Analysis [1934].* USA: McGraw-Hill Education, 2008.

Cornell, Joseph W. *Spin-Off to Pay-Off: An Analytical Guide to Investing in Corporate Divestitures.* New York: McGraw-Hill, 1998.

Hagstrom, Robert G. *Investing: The Last Liberal Art.* New York: Columbia Business School Publishing, 2013.

Hagstrom, Robert G. *The Warren Buffet Way: Investment Strategies of the World's Greatest Investor.* USA: John Wiley & Sons, 1995.

Kass, Doug. *Doug Kass on the Market: A life on TheStreet.* New Jersey: Wiley & Sons, 2014.

Koller, Tim, McKinsey & Company Inc., Mark Goedhart and David Wessels. *Valuation: Measuring and Managing the Value of Companies (6th edition).* New Jersey: John Wiley & Sons, 2015.

Kemp, Michael. *Uncommon Sense: Investment Wisdom since the Stock Market's Dawn.* Melbourne: John Wiley & Sons Australia, 2016.

Klarman, Seth A. *Margin of Safety: Risk Averse Value Investing Strategies for the Thoughtful Investor.* USA: Harper Business Publishers, 1991.

Krass, Peter. *The Book of Investing Wisdom: Classic Writings by Great Stock-Pickers and Legends of Wall Street.* New Jersey: John Wiley & Sons, 1999.

Lefèvre, Edwin. *Reminiscences of a Stock Operator [1923].* New Jersey: John Wiley & Sons, 1993.

Lev, Baruch and Feng Gu. *The End of Accounting and the Path Forward for Investors and Managers.* New Jersey: John Wiley & Sons, 2016.

Livermore, Jesse. *How to Trade in Stocks [1940].* USA: McGraw-Hill, 2001.USA: Trader's Press, 2001.

Loeb, Gerald M. *The Battle for Investment Survival.* USA: John Wiley & Sons, 1996.

Lynch, Peter and John Rothchild. *One Up on Wall Street: How to Use What You Already Know to Make Money in the Market.* New York: Fireside, 1989.

Mauldin, John and Worth Wray. *A Great Leap Forward?: Making Sense of China's Cooling Credit Boom, Technological Transformation, High Stakes Rebalancing, Geopolitical Rise, & Reserve Currency Dream.* Mauldin Economics, 2015.

Mauldin, John. *Just One Thing: Twelve of the World's Best Investors Reveal the One Strategy You Can't Overlook.* New Jersey: John Wiley & Sons, 2006.

Mayer, Christopher W. *100 Baggers: Stocks That Return 100-to-1 and How to Find Them.* USA: Laissez Faire Books, 2015.

Mihaljevic, John. *The Manual of Ideas: The Proven Framework for Finding the Best Value Investments.* USA: John Wiley & Sons, 2013.

Neff, John. *John Neff on Investing.* USA: John Wiley & Sons, 1999.

Neill, Humphrey B. *The Art of Contrary Thinking.* USA: Caxton Printers, 1954.

Phelps, Thomas W. *100 to 1 in the Stock Market: A Distinguished Security Analyst Tells How to Make More of Your Investment Opportunities [1972]*. USA: Echo Point Books, 2014.

Rogers, Jim. *Adventure Capitalist: The Ultimate Road Trip*. New York: Random House, 2003.

Rothchild, David. *The Davis Dynasty: Fifty Years of Successful Investing on Wall Street*. USA: John Wiley & Sons, 2001.

Schwager, Jack D. *Hedge Fund Market Wizards: How Winning Traders Win*. New Jersey, John Wiley & Sons, 2012.

Schwager, Jack D. *Market Wizards: Interviews with Top Traders*. New York: Simon & Schuster, 1989.

Schwager, Jack D. *Stock Market Wizards: Interviews with America's Top Stock Traders*. USA: HarperCollins Books, 2001.

Schwed, Fred. *Where Are the Customer's Yachts? Or A Good Look at Wall Street*. New Jersey: John Wiley & Sons, 1940.

Sears, Steven M. *The Indomitable Investor: Why a Few Succeed in the Stock Market When Everyone Else Fails*. New Jersey: John Wiley & Sons, 2012.

Sharma, Ruchir. *The Rise and Fall of Nations: Forces of Change in the Post-Crisis World.* USA: W. W. Norton & Company, 2016.

Shearn, Michael. *The Investment checklist: The Art of In-Depth Research.* USA: John Wiley & Sons, 2012.

Spier, Guy. *The Education of a Value Investor: My Transformative Quest for Wealth, Wisdom, and Enlightenment.* USA: St. Martin's Press, 2014.

Swensen, David F. *Pioneering Portfolio Management: An Unconventional Approach to Institutional Investment.* USA: Free Press, 2000.

Szpiro, George G. *Pricing the Future: Finance, Physics, and the 300-year Journey to the Black-Scholes Equation.* New York: Perseus Book Group, 2011.

Tetlock, Philip E. and Dan Gardner. *Superforecasting: The Art and Science of Prediction.* USA: Broadway Books, 2015.

Thorndike, William N. *The Outsiders: Eight Unconventional CEOs and Their Radically Rational Blueprint for Success.* USA: Harvard Business School Publishing, 2012.

Tillinghast, Joel. *Big Money Thinks Small: Biases, Blind Spots, and Smarter Investing.* New York: Columbia University Press, 2017.

Vliet, Pim Van and Jan De Koning. *High Returns from Low Risk: A Remarkable Stock Market Paradox*. United Kingdom: John Wiley & Sons, 2017.

Ware, Jim and Jim Dethmer, with Jamie Ziegler and Fran Skinner. *High Performing Investment Teams: How to Achieve Best Practices of Top Firms.* USA: John Wiley & Sons, 2006.

Business Management

Cunningham, Lawrence and Warren Buffett. *The Essays of Warren Buffett: Lessons for Corporate America*. USA: The Cunningham Group & Carolina Academic Press, 2015.

Doerr, Jon and Kris Duggan. *Measure What Matters: How Bono, the Gates Foundation, and Google Rock the World with OKRs*. New York: Penguin Publishing Group, 2017.

Greenwald, Bruce C. and Judd Kahn *Competition Demystified: A Radically Simplified Approach to Business Strategy*. New York: Penguin Group, 2005.

Heath, Chip and Dan Heath. *The Power of Moments: Why Certain Experiences Have Extraordinary Impact*. New York: Simon and Schuster, 2017.

Horowitz, Ben. *The Hard Thing About Hard Things: Building a Business When There Are No Easy Answers.* New York: Harper Collins, 2014.

Iverson, Ken. *Plain Talk: Lessons from a Business Maverick.* USA: John Wiley & Sons, 1998.

Lipp, Doug. *Disney U: How Disney University Develops the World's Most Engaged, Loyal, and Customer-Centric Employees.* USA: McGraw-Hill, 2013.

Marquet, L. David. *Turn the Ship Around!: A True Story of Turning Followers into Leaders.* USA: Penguin, 2012.

Mello, Francisco Souza. *The 3G Way: An Introduction to the Management Style of the Trio Who's Taken Some of the Most Important Icons in American Capitalism.* USA: 10x Books, 2015.

Newport, Cal. *Deep Work: Rules for Focused Success in a Distracted World.* New York: Grand Central Publishing, 2016.

Porter, Michael E. *Competitive Strategy: Techniques for Analyzing Industries and Competitors.* New York: The Free Press, 1980.

Segall, Ken. *Insanely Simple: The Obsession That Drives Apple's Success.* New York: Penguin, 2012.

Stulberg, Brad and Steve Magness. *Peak Performance: Elevate Your Game, Avoid Burnout, and Thrive with the New Science of Success*. New York: Rodale, 2017.

Zook, Chris and James Allen. *The Founder's Mentality: How to Overcome the Predictable Crisis of Growth*. USA: Bain & Company, 2016.

Moon, Youngme. *Different: Escaping the Competitive Herd*. New York: Crown Business, 2010.

Companies

Accenture. *Values. Driven. Leadership: The History of Accenture*. Virginia: The History Factory, 2005.

Buffett, Warren and Max Olson. *Berkshire Hathaway Letters to Shareholders 1965-2017*. USA: Explorist Productions, 2018.

Chutkow, Paul. *Visa: The Power of an Idea*. Chicago: Harcourt, 2001.

Clark, Duncan. *Alibaba: The House That Jack Ma Built*. New York: Harper Collins, 2016.

Coll, Steve. *Private Empire: ExxonMobil and American Power*. New York: Penguin, 2012.

Ellis, Charles D. *The Partnership: The Making of Goldman Sachs*. New York: Penguin, 2008.

Galloway, Scott. *The Four: The Hidden DNA of Amazon, Apple, Facebook, and Google*. New York: Penguin, 2017.

Kirk, Margaret O. *Orkin: The Making of The World's Best Pest Control Company*. USA: Rollins Inc, 2005.

McDonald, Duff. *The Firm: The Story of McKinsey and Its Secret Influence on American Business*. New York: Simon and Schuster, 2014.

Schultz, Howard and Joanne Gordon. *Onward: How Starbucks Fought for Its Life Without Losing its Soul*. USA: Rodale Books, 2011.

Schmidt, Eric and Johnathan Rosenberg. *How Google Works*. Grand Central Publishing, 2014.

Stenebo, John. *The Truth About Ikea: The Secret Behind the World's Fifth Richest Man and the Success of the Swedish Flatpack Giant*. Great Britain: Gibson Square Books, 2010.

Stone, Brad. *The Everything Store: Jeff Bezos and the Age of Amazon*. USA: Little, Brown and Company, 2014.

Stuart, James B. *DisneyWar: The Battle for the Magic Kingdom*. Great Britain: Simon & Schuster, 2006.

Terry, Bob. *Honest Weight: The Story of Toledo Scale*. USA: Xlibris Corporation, 2000.

Biographies

Adams, Scott. *How to Fail at Almost Everything and Still Win Big: Kind of the Story of My Life*. New York: Penguin, 2013.

Benioff, Marc R. *Behind the Cloud: The Untold Story of How Salesforce.com went from Idea to Billion-Dollar Company – and Revolutionized the Industry.* San Francisco: Jossey-Bass, 2009.

Bhanver, Jagmohan. *Pichai: The Future of Google. India*: Hachette India, 2016.

Cannadine, David. *Mellon: An American Life.* New York: Random House, 2006.

Cardoso, Fernando Henrique. *The Accidental President of Brazil: A Memoir.* USA: Public Affairs, 2007.

Chernow, Ron. *Titan: The Life of John D. Rockefeller, Sr.* New York: Random House, 1988.

Chernow, Ron. *Washington: A Life.* USA: Penguin, 2010.

200

Chernow, Ron. *Alexander Hamilton*. USA: Penguin, 2014.

Correia, Cristiane. *Dream Big: How the Brazilian Trio Behind 3G – Jorge Paulo Lemann, Marcel Telles and Beto Sicupira Acquired Anheuser-Busch, Burger King and Heinz*. Sextante, 2014.

Dalio, Ray. *Principles: Life and Work*. New York: Simonb & Schuster, 2017.

Davis, Seth. *Wooden: A Coach's Life*. New York: Henry Holt & Company, 2014.

Derman, Emanuel. *My Life as a Quant: Reflections on Physics and Finance*. New Jersey: John Wiley & Sons, 2004.

Duff, Turney. *The Buy Side: A Wall Street Trader's Tale of Spectacular Excess*. New York: Random House, 2013.

Feynman, Richard. *Surely You're Joking, Mr. Feynman! (Adventures of a Curious Character)*. USA: Norton Paperback, 1997.

Grant, James. *Bernard Baruch: The Adventures of a Wall Street Legend*. USA: John Wiley & Sons, 1997.

Henriques, Diana B. *The Wizard of Lies: Bernie Madoff and the Death of Trust*. New York: St. Martin's Press, 2011.

Isaacson, Walter. *Albert Einstein: His Life and Universe*. New York: Simon & Schuster, 2007.

Isaacson, Walter. *Benjamin Franklin: An American Life*. New York: Simon & Schuster, 2003.

Isaacson, Walter. *Steve Jobs*. New York: Simon & Schuster, 2011.

Kasparov, Garry. *Deep Thinking: Where Machine Intelligence Ends and Human Creativity Begins*. New York: Public Affairs, 2017.

Kaufman, Michael T. *Soros: The Life and Times of a Messianic Billionaire*. New York: Random House, 2002.

Knight, Phil. *Shoe Dog: A Memoir by the Creator of Nike*. USA: Scribner, 2016.

Kolhatkar, Sheelah. *Black Edge: Inside Information, Dirty Money, and the Quest to Bring Down the Most Wanted Man on Wall Street*. New York: Random House, 2017.

Kroc, Ray. *Grinding It Out: The Making of McDonald's*. New York: St. Martin's Press, 2016.

Langone, Ken. *I Love Capitalism!: An American Story*. New York: Penguin, 2018.

Levy, Leon and Eugene Linden. *The Mind of Wall Street: A Legendary Financier on the Perils of Greed and the Mysteries of the Market*. USA: Perseus Books, 2002.

Lewis, Michael. *The Undoing Project: A Friendship that Changed Our Minds*. New York: W. W. Norton & Company, 2017.

Loomis, Carol J. *Tap Dancing to Work: Warren Buffett on Practically Everything, 1966-2013*. New York: Penguin, 2012.

Lowe, Janet. *Damn Right!* USA: John Wiley & Sons, 2000.

McLamore, James W. *The Burger King: Jim McLamore and the Building of an Empire*. New York: McGraw-Hill, 1998.

Mirchandani, Dilip. *One Way Up Wall Street: The Fred Alger Story*. USA: James Charlton Associates, 1999.

Moore, Kenny. *Bowerman and the Men of Oregon: The Story of Oregon's Legendary Coach and Nike's Cofounder*. USA: Rodale Inc., 2006.

Mouton, Jannie. *And Then They Fired Me*. South Africa: Tafelberg Publishers, 2011.

Munger, Charles T. *Poor Charlie's Almanack: The Wit and Wisdom of Charles T. Munger, Volume 3.* Virginia: The Donning Company Publishers, 2006.

Partnoy, Frank. *The Match King: Ivar Kreuger, The Financial Genius Behind a Century of Wall Street Scandals.* USA: Public Affairs, 2009.

Pickens, T. Boone. *The First Billion is the Hardest: Reflections on a Life of Comebacks and America's Energy Future.* New York: Random House, 2008.

Pifer, Drury L. *Hanging the Moon: The Rollins Rise to Riches.* New Jersey: University Delaware Press, 2001.

Rempel, William C. *The Gambler: How Penniless Dropout Kirk Kerkorian Became the Greatest Deal Maker in Capitalist History.* New York: Harper Collins, 2018.

Renehan, Edward J. *Dark Genius of Wall Street: The Misunderstood Life of Jay Gould, King of the Robber Barons.* USA: Perseus Books, 2005.

Rubin, Robert E. and Jacob Weisberg. *In an Uncertain World: Tough Choices from Wall Street to Washington.* New York: Random House, 2004.

Rubython, Tom. *Jesse Livermore - Boy Plunger: The Man Who Sold America Short in 1929.* USA: The Myrtle Press, 2015.

Schnatter, John H. *Papa: The Story of Papa John's Pizza*. USA: Koehler Books, 2017.

Schroeder, Alice. *Snowball: Warren Buffett and the Business of Life*. USA: Bantam Books, 2009.

Segal, Gillian Zoe. *Getting There: A Book of Mentors*. USA: Harry N. Abrams, 2015.

Smitten, Richard. *Jesse Livermore: The World's Greatest Stock Trader*. USA: John Wiley & Sons, 2001.

Soros, George. *Soros on Soros: Staying Ahead of the Curve*. USA: John Wiley & Sons, 1995.

Stevens, Mark. *King Icahn: A Biography of a Renegade Capitalist.* New York: Penguin, 1993.

Strachman, Daniel A. *Julian Robertson: A Tiger in the Land of Bulls and Bears*. USA: John Wiley & Sons, 2004.

Sykes, Timothy. *An American Hedge Fund: How I Made $2 Million as a Stock Operator & Created a Hedge Fund*. USA: Bullship Press, 2008.

Thorp, Edward O. *A Man for All Markets: From Las Vegas to Wall Street, How I Beat the Dealer and the Market*. New York: Random House Publishing Group, 2017.

Vance, Ashlee. *Elon Musk: Tesla, SpaceX, and the Quest for a Fantastic Future*. USA: HarperCollins, 2015.

Vincent, Isabel. *Gilded Lily: Lily Safra: The Making of One of the World's Wealthiest Widows*. New York: Harper Collins, 2011.

Walton, Sam. *Sam Walton: Made In America*. New York: Random House Publishing Group, 2012.

Zell, Sam. *Am I Being Too Subtle?: Straight Talk From a Business Rebel*. New York: Penguin, 2017.

Zuckoff, Mitchell. *Ponzi's Scheme: The True Story of a Financial Legend*. New York: Random House, 2005.

History

Ahamed, Liaquat. *Lords of Finance: The Bankers Who Broke the World*. New York: Penguin, 2009.

Allen, Frederick Lewis. *Only Yesterday: An Informal History of the 1920s*. New York: Harper Perennial, 1931.

Allen, Frederick Lewis. *Since Yesterday: The 1930s in America, September 3, 1929–September 3, 1939*. New York: Harper Perennial, 1940.

Allen, Frederick Lewis. *The Big Change: America Transforms Itself: 1900-1950*. New York: Harper & Brothers, 1952.

Bernstein, Peter L. *The Power of Gold: The History of an Obsession*. New York: John Wiley & Sons, 2000.

Biggs, Barton. *Wealth, War & Wisdom*. New Jersey: John Wiley & Sons, 2008.

Braziel, E. Russel. *The Domino Effect*. Madison, WI: CWL Publishing Enterprise, 2016.

Brooks, John. *Business Adventures: Twelve Classic Tales from the World of Wall Street*. New York: Open Road Integration Media, 1959.

Brooks, John. *The Go-Go Years: The Drama and Crashing Finale of Wall Street's Bullish 60s*. New Jersey: John Wiley, 1973.

Carey, David and John E. Morris. *King of Capital. The Remarkable Rise, Fall, and Rise Again of Steve Schwarzman and Blackstone*. USA: Crown Business, 2010.

Chancellor, Edward. *Devil Take the Hindmost: A History of Financial Speculation*. New York: Penguin Press, 1999.

Chernow, Ron. *The House of Morgan: An American Banking Dynasty and the Rise of Modern Finance*.

Cohan, William D. *House of Cards: A Tale of Hubris and Wretched Excess on Wall Street*. New York: Random House, 2009.

Constantine, Lloyd. *Priceless: The Case that Brought Down the Visa/MasterCard Bank Cartel*. New York: Kaplan Publishing, 2009.

Cooper, Andrew S. *The Oil Kings: How the U.S., Iran, and Saudi Arabia Changed the Balance of Power in the Middle East*. New York: Simon and Schuster, 2011.

de la Vega, Joseph. *Confusion de Confusiones [1688]*. USA: John Wiley & Sons, 1996.

Dalio, Ray. *Big Debt Crisis*. Connecticut: Bridgewater, 2018.

Durant, Will and Ariel Durant. *The Lessons of History: The celebrated collection of essays compiling over 5000 years of history by two of the greatest attesters of our time*. New York: Simon and Schuster, 2012.

Ferguson, Niall. *The Ascent of Money: A Financial History of the World*. New York: Penguin, 2008.

Fergusson, Adam. *When Money Dies: The Nightmare of Deficit Spending, Devaluation, and Hyperinflation in Weimar Germany*. USA: Public Affairs, 1975.

Fischer, David H. *The Great Wave: Price Revolutions and the Rhythm of History.* New York: Oxford University Press, 1996.

Freeman, Joshua B. *Behemoth: A History of the Factory and the Making of the Modern World.* New York: W. W. Norton & Company, 2018.

Friedman, George. *The Next 100 Years: A Forecast for the 21st Century.* New York: Random House, 2009.

Friedman, Milton. *Money Mischief: Episodes in Monetary History.* USA: Houghton Mifflin Harcourt Publishing Company, 1992.

Friedman, Milton and Anna J. Schwartz. *A Monetary History of the United States (1867-1960).* USA: Princeton University Press, 1963.

Friedman, Milton and Anna J. Schwartz. *The Great Contraction, 1923-1933 (Princeton Classic Edition).* New Jersey: Princeton University Press, 1963.

Galbraith, John. *The Great Crash 1929.* USA: Houghton Mifflin Harcourt Publishing Company, 1954.

Gordon, John S. *The Great Game: The Emergence of Wall Street as a World Power (1953-2000):* New York: Touchstone, 1999.

Grant, James. *Mr. Market Miscalculates: The Bubble Years and Beyond.* USA: Axios Press, 2008.

Grant, James. *The Trouble with Prosperity: The Loss of Fear, the Rise of Speculation and the risk to American Savings.* New York: Random House, 1996.

Greenblatt, Stephen. *The Swerve: How the World Became Modern.* New York: W. W. Norton & Company, 2011.

Harari, Yuval N. *Sapiens: A Brief History of Mankind.* New York: Harper Collins, 2015.

Harberler, Gottfried V. *Prosperity and Depression: A Theoretical Analysis of Cyclical Movements [1937].* USA: University Press of the Pacific, 2001.

Hawking, Stephen. *A Brief History of Time.* USA: Bantam Books, 1988.

Homer, Sidney and Richard Sylla. *A History of Interest Rates.* New York: John Wiley & Sons, 2011.

Isaacson, Walter. *The Innovators: How a Group of Hackers, Geniuses, and Geeks Created the Digital Revolution.* New York: Simon & Schuster, 2014.

Jonnes, Jill. *Conquering Gotham. Building Penn Station and its Tunnels.* New York: Penguin Group, 2007.

Kindleberger, Charles P. and Robert Aliber. *Manias, Panics, and Crashes: A History of Financial Crisis*. USA: John Wiley & Sons, 1978.

Levinson, Marc. *The Box: How the Shipping Container Made the World Smaller and the World Economy Bigger*. United Kingdom: Princeton University Press, 2016.

Lewis, Michael. *Boomerang: Travels in the New Third World*. New York: W. W. Norton & Company, 2011.

Lewis, Michael. *Flash Boys: A Wall Street Revolt*. New York: W. W. Norton & Company, 2014.

Lewis, Michael. *Liar's Poker*. New York: W. W. Norton & Company, 1989.

Lewis, Michael. *Panic! The Story of Modern Financial Insanity*. USA: The Courier Companies, 2009.

Lewis, Michael. *The Big Short: Inside the Doomsday Machine*. New York: W. W. Norton & Company, 2010.

Lowenstein, Roger. *When Genius Failed: The Rise and Fall of Long-Term Capital Management*. New York: Random House, 2000.

Lowenstein, Roger. *While America Aged: How Pension Debts Ruined General Motors, Stopped the NYC Subways, Bankrupted San Diego, and Loom as the Next Financial Crisis.* USA: Penguin Press, 2008.

Mackay, Charles. *Extraordinary Popular Delusions and The Madness of Crowds (1841).* USA: John Wiley & Sons, 1996.

Malkiel, Burton G. *A Random Walk Down Wall Street: The Time-Tested Strategy for Successful Investing.* USA: W. W. Norton & Company, 1990.

Mamis, Justin. *When to Sell: Inside Strategies for Stock-Market Profits.* USA: Fraser Publishing Company, 1994.

Mantle, Jonathan. *Car Wars: Fifty Years of Backstabbing, Infighting, and Industrial Espionage in the Global Market.* USA: Arcade Publishing, 1995.

McCullough, David. *1776.* New York: Simon & Schuster, 2005.

McGrayne, Sharon B. *The Theory that Would Not Die: How Bayes' Rule Cracked the Enigma Code, Hunted Down Russian Submarines, and Emerged Triumphant from Two Centuries of Controversy.* USA: Yale University Press, 2011.

Mlodinow, Leonard. *Euclid's Window: The Story of Geometry from Parallel Lines to Hyperspace.* New York: Touchstone, 2001.

Nocera, Joe. *A Piece of the Action: How the Middle Class Joined the Money Class.* USA: Simon & Schuster, 1994.

Partnoy, Frank. *Infectious Greed: How Deceit and Risk Corrupted the Financial Markets.* USA: Henry Holt & Company, 2003.

Patterson, Scott. *The Quants: How a New Breed of Math Whizzes Conquered Wall Street and Nearly Destroyed It.* New York: Random House, 2010.

Poundstone, William. *Fortune's Formula: The Untold Story of the Scientific Betting System That Beat the Casinos and Wall Street.* New York: Farrar, Straus and Giroux, 2005.

Raghavan, Anita. *The Billionaire's Apprentice: The Rise of the Indian-American Elite and the Fall of The Galleon Hedge Fund.* USA: Business Plus, 2013.

Reinhart, Carmen M. and Kenneth S. Rogoff. *This Time is Different: Eight Centuries of Financial Folly.* USA: Princeton University Press, 2009.

Remini, Robert V. *A Short History of the United States: From the Arrival of Native American Tribes to the Obama Presidency.* USA: Harper Perennial, 2009.

Ridley, Matt. *The Evolution of Everything: How New Ideas Emerge*. USA: Harper Perennial, 2016.

Ridley, Matt. *The Rational Optimist: How Prosperity Evolves*. USA: HarperCollins Publishers, 2010.

Roberts, J. M. *History of the World, Updated*. England: Oxford University Press, 2013.

Rothbard, Murray N. *America's Great Depression*. USA: The Ludwig von Mises Institute, 1963.

Rudolph, Richard. *The Tedious, Brief History of Insurance*. USA: The National Alliance Research Academy, 2015.

Shlaes, Amity. *The Forgotten Man: A New History of the Great Depression*. USA: Harper Press, 2007.

Shlaes, Amity. *Coolidge*. New York: Harper Collins Publisher, 2013.

Wessel, David. *In Fed We Trust: Ben Bernanke's War on the Great Panic – How the Federal Reserve Became the Fourth Branch of Government*. USA: Three Rivers Press, 2009.

Soros, George. *The Crash of 2008 and What it Means: The New Paradigm for Financial Markets*. New York: Public Affairs, 2008.

Standiford, Les. *Meet You in Hell: Andrew Carnegie, Henry Clay Frick, and the Bitter Partnership That Transformed America*. New York: Random House, 2005.

Strauss, Willian and Neil Howe. *The Fourth Turning: What the Cycles of History Tell Us About America's Next Rendezvous with Destiny*. New York: Crown/Archetype, 2009.

Womack, James P., Daniel T. Jones, and Daniel Roos. *The Machine That Changed the World: The Story of Lean Production – Toyota's Secret Weapon in the Global Car Wars*. USA: Harper Perennial, 1991.

Wood, Christopher. *The Bubble Economy: Japan's Extraordinary Speculative Boom of the '80s and the Dramatic Bust of the '90s*. USA: Solstice Publishing, 1993.

Yergin, Daniel. *The Quest: Energy, Security, and the Remaking of the Modern World Industry*. USA: Penguin Books, 2011.

Psychology

Achor, Shawn. *The Happiness Advantage: How a Positive Brain Fuels Success in Work and Life*. New York: Penguin Random House, 2010.

Adams, Scott. *Win Bigly: Persuasion in a World Where Facts Don't Matter*. New York: Penguin, 2017.

Carnegie, Dale. *How to Win Friends & Influence People*. New York: Simon & Schuster, 1936.

Cialdini, Robert B. *Influence: The Psychology of Persuasion*. New York: Harper Collins, 1993.

Colvin, Geoff. *Talent is Overrated: What Really Separates World-Class Performers from Everybody Else*. New York: Penguin, 2010.

Dwek, Carol S. *Mindset: The New Psychology of Success*. New York: Penguin Random House, 2006.

Gardner, Daniel. *Future Babble: Why Pundits Are Hedgehogs and Foxes Know Best*. USA: McClelland & Stewart Ltd, 2010.

Holiday, Ryan. *Ego is the Enemy*. New York: Penguin, 2016.

Holmes, Jamie. *Nonsense: The Power of Not Knowing*. New York: Broadway Books, 2015.

Le Bon, Gustave. *The Crowd: A Study of the Popular Mind [1895]*. USA: Dover Publications, 2002.

Mauboussin, Michael J. *Think Twice. Harnessing the Power of Counterintuition.* USA: Harvard Business School Publishing, 2009.

McArdle, Megan. *The Upside of Down: Why Failing Well Is the Key to Success.* New York: Penguin Books, 2014.

McGonigal, Kelly. *The Willpower Instinct: How Self-Control Works, Why It Matters, and What You Can Do to Get More of It.* New York: Penguin, 2012.

Nofsinger, John. *The Psychology of Investing.* USA: Pearson Prentice Press, 2002.

Peterson, Jordan B. *12 Rules for Life: An Antidote to Chaos.* Canada: Random House, 2018.

Peterson, Richard L. *Inside the Investor's Brain: The Power of Mind Over Money.* USA: John Wiley & Sons, 2007.

Rosenberg, Marshall. *Nonviolent Communication: A Language of Life, 3rd Edition: Life-Changing Tools for Healthy Relationships.* New York: PuddleDancer Press, 2015.

Runkel, Hal. *Screamfree Parenting, 10th Anniversary Revised Edition: How to Raise Amazing Adults by Learning to Pause More and React Less.* New York: Random House, 2007.

Siegel, Daniel, M.D. *Aware: The Science and Practice of Presence--The Groundbreaking Meditation Practice.* New York: Penguin, 2018.

Stephens-Davidowitz, Seth. *Everybody Lies: Big Data, New Data, and What the Internet Can Tell Us About Who We Really Are.* New York: Harper Collins, 2017.

Tan, Chade-Meng and Daniel Goleman. *Search Inside Yourself: The Unexpected Path to Achieving Success, Happiness (and World Peace).* New York: Harper Collins, 2012.

Tan, Chade-Meng. *Joy on Demand: The Art of Discovering the Happiness Within.* New York: Harper Collins, 2016.

Sociology

Brooks, Arthur C. *The Road to Freedom: How to Win the Fight for Free Enterprise.* USA: Basic Books, 2012.

Bush, Jonathan and Stephen Baker. *Where Does it Hurt?: An Entrepreneur's Guide to Fixing Health Care.* New York: Penguin, 2014.

Fleckenstein, William and Frederick Sheehan. *Greenspan's Bubbles: The Age of Ignorance at the Federal Reserve*. USA: McGraw-Hill, 2008.

Murray, Charles. *Coming Apart: The State of White America*. USA: Cox and Murray, 2012.

Rosling, Hans. *Factfulness: Ten Reasons We're Wrong About the World--and Why Things Are Better Than You Think*. New York: Flatiron Books, 2018.

Philosophy

Berlin, Isaiah. *The Hedgehog and the Fox: An Essay on Tolstoy's View of History*. USA: Elephant Paperbacks, 1953.

Dawkins, Richard. *The Magic of Reality: How We Know What's Really True*. New York: Free Press, 2012.

La Rochefoucauld. *Maxims [1613-1680]*. USA: St. Augustine Press, 2009.

Lama, Dalai. *The Art of Happiness: A Handbook for Living*. New York: Penguin Putnam, 1998.

Pinker, Steven. *Enlightenment Now: The Case for Reason, Science, Humanism, and Progress*. New York: Penguin, 2018.

Taleb, Nassim Nicholas. *The Bed of Procrustes: Philosophical and Practical Aphorisms.* New York: Random House, 2010.

Manson, Mark. *The Subtle Art of Not Giving a F*ck: A Counterintuitive Approach to Living a Good Life.* USA: Harper One, 2016.

Soros, George. *The Alchemy of Finance.* USA: John Wiley & Sons, 1987.

Taleb, Nassim Nicholas. *Fooled by Randomness: The Hidden Role of Chance in Life and in the Markets.* New York: Random House, 2004.

Natural Sciences

Carroll, Sean. *The Big Picture: On the Origins of Life, Meaning, and the Universe Itself.* New York: Penguin, 2016.

Eliot, Lise. *What's Going on in There?: How the Brain and Mind Develop in the First Five Years of Life.* USA: Bantom Books, 1999.

Johnson, Steven. *Where Good Ideas Come from: The Natural History of Innovation.* New York: Penguin, 2010.

Lucretius. *On the Nature of Things [1st Century B.C.].* USA: Henry Regnery Company, 1949.

Shlain, Leonard. *Leonardo's Brain: Understanding da Vinci's Creative Genius.* England: Lyon's Press, 2014.

Technology

Auletta, Ken. *Frenemies: The Epic Disruption of the Ad Business (and Everything Else).* New York: Penguin Press, 2018.

Berleant, Daniel. *The Race to the Future: What Could Happen – and What to Do.* USA: Lifeboat Foundation Publications, 2013.

Bryce, Robert. *Power Hungry: The Myths of "Green" Energy and the Real Fuels of the Future.* USA: Public Affairs, 2010.

Brynjolfsson, Erik and Andrew McAfee. *Race Against the Machine: How the Digital Revolution is Accelerating Innovation, Driving Productivity, and Irreversibly Transforming Employment and the Economy.* USA: Digital Frontier Press, 2011.

Brynjolfsson, Erik and Andrew McAfee. *Machine, Platform, Crowd: Harnessing Our Digital Future.* USA: W. W. Norton & Company, 2017.

Ford, Martin. *Rise of the Robots: Technology and the Threat of a Jobless Future.* USA: Perseus Books, 2015.

Sundararajan, Arun. *The Sharing Economy: The End of Employment and the Rise of Crowd-Based Capitalism.* Cambridge, MA: MIT Press, 2016.

Tzuo, Tien and Gabe Weisert. *Subscribed: Why the Subscription Model Will Be Your Company's Future - and What to Do About It.* New York: Penguin, 2018.

Economics

Akerlof, George and Robert Shiller. *Phishing for Phools: The Economics of Manipulation and Deception.* New Jersey: Princeton University Press, 2015.

El-Erian, Mohamed A. *The Only Game in Town: Central Banks, Instability, and Avoiding the Next Collapse.* New York: Random House, 2016.

Axelrod, Robert. *The Evolution of Cooperation.* Cambridge, MA: Basic Books, 1984.

Hayek, Friedrich A. *The Road to Serfdom.* Routledge, London: The University of Chicago Press, 1944.

Koo, Richard. *The Holy Grail of Macro Economics: Lessons from Japan's Great Recession.* USA: John Wiley & Sons, 2009.

Mauldin, John and Jonathan Tepper. *Endgame: The End of the Debt Supercycle and How It Changes Everything*. New Jersey: John Wiley & Sons, 2011.

Minsky, Hyman P. *John Maynard Keynes*. USA: Columbia University Press, 2008.

Mises, Ludwig von. *Planned Chaos*. USA: Ludwig Von Mises Institute, 2009.

Moazed, Alex and Nicholas L. Johnson. *Modern Monopolies: What It Takes to Dominate the 21st Century Economy*. New York: St. Martin's Press, 2016.

Rogoff, Kenneth S. *The Curse of Cash*. New Jersey: Princeton University Press, 2016.

Schelling, Thomas. *Micro Motives and Macro Behavior*. USA: W. W. Norton & Company, 1978.

Schlichter, Detlev S. *Paper Money Collapse: The Folly of Elastic Money and the Coming Monetary Breakdown*. USA: John Wiley & Sons, 2011.

Smith, Adam. *The Wealth of Nations [1776]*. USA: Modern Library, 2000.

Miscellaneous

Christensen, Clayton, James Allworth and Karen Dillon. *How Will You Measure Your Life?* New York: Harper Collins, 2012.

Colvin, Geoff. *Talent is Overrated: What Really Separates World-Class Performers from Everybody Else.* New York: Penguin, 2010.

Cuadros, Alex. *Brazillionaires: Wealth, Power, Decadence, and Hope in an American Country.* New York: Penguin Random House, 2016.

Dent Jr., Harry S. *The Demographics Cliff: How to Survive and Prosper During the Great Deflation of 2014-2019.* New York: Penguin, 2014.

Ferris, Timothy. *Tools of Titans: The Tactics, Routines, and Habits of Billionaires, Icons, and World-Class Performers.* New York: Houghton Mifflin Harcourt Publishing Company, 2017.

Friedman, George. *Flashpoints: The Emerging Crisis in Europe.* New York: Penguin, 2015.

Gates Sr., Bill and Mary A. Mackin. *Showing Up for Life: Thoughts on the Gifts of a Lifetime.* New York: Broadway Books, 2009.

Gawande, Atul. *Being Mortal: Medicine and What Matters in the End*. New York: Metropolitan Books, 2014.

Gawande, Atul. *The Checklist Manifesto: How to Get Things Right*. New York: Metropolitan books, 2009.

Gladwell, Malcolm. *David and Goliath: Underdogs, Misfits, and the Art of Battling Giants*. New York: Little, Brown and Company Hachette Book Group, 2013.

Gladwell, Malcolm. *Outliers: The Story of Success*. New York: Little, Brown and Company Hachette Book Group, 2008.

Gladwell, Malcolm. *The Tipping Point: How Little Things Can Make a Big Difference*. New York: Little, Brown and Company Hachette Book Group, 2000.

Greene, Robert. *48 Laws of Power*. New York: Penguin, 2000.

Greene, Robert. *Mastery*. New York, Penguin, 2012.

Kissinger, Henry. *On China*. New York: Penguin Books, 2011.

Lewis, Michael. *Moneyball: The Art of Winning an Unfair Game*. W. W. Norton & Company, 2003.

Machiavelli, Niccolo. *The Prince [1532].* USA: Dover Publications, 1992.

Miller, Alan B. *Health Care Reform That Makes Sense: A Detailed Plan to Improve the Health Care System by America's Leading Health Care CEO.* New York: Sterling & Ros Publishers, 2009.

Pollan, Michael. *How to Change Your Mind: What the New Science of Psychedelics Teaches Us About Consciousness, Dying, Addiction, Depression, and Transcendence.* New York: Penguin, 2018.

Rand, Ayn. *Atlas Shrugged.* New York: Penguin, 1957.

Ringer, Robert. *Looking Out for #1: How to Get from Where You Are Now to Where You Want to Be in Life.* USA: Skyhorse Publishing, 2013.

Schiff, Lewis. *Business Brilliant: Surprising Lessons from the Greatest Self-Made Business Icons.* USA: HarperCollins, 2013.

Tzu, Sun. *The Art of War [1581].* USA: Filiquarian Publishing, 2006.

Wilson, Richard C. *The Family Office Book: Investing Capital for the Ultra-Affluent.* New Jersey: John Wiley & Sons, 2012.

Made in the USA
Coppell, TX
09 December 2020

44045310R00132